HOW TO PUBLISH A BOOK ON AMAZON

THE ULTIMATE GUIDE TO KINDLE DIRECT PUBLISHING

NINA HARRINGTON

HOW TO PUBLISH A BOOK ON AMAZON

THE ULTIMATE GUIDE TO KINDLE DIRECT PUBLISHING

NINA HARRINGTON

FAST-TRACK GUIDES

FOCUSED TRAINING FOR AUTHORS

FAST-TRACK GUIDES

FOCUSED TRAINING FOR AUTHORS

HOW TO PUBLISH A BOOK ON AMAZON

The Ultimate Guide to Kindle Direct Publishing

COPYRIGHT© 2020 NINA HARRINGTON

https://ninaharrington.com/

CONTENTS

PART THREE. HOW TO USE THE KINDLE CREATE TOOL TO FORMAT AND PUBLISH EBOOKS AND PRINT BOOKS

PART FOUR. YOUR AMAZON AUTHOR PAGE

PART FIVE. BOX SETS

INTRODUCTION

If you are an author who dreams of sharing your work online to a worldwide audience, without the support of a literary agent or a traditional publishing house, then Amazon Kindle Direct Publishing (KDP) is for you.

Using the Amazon Kindle Direct Publishing platform, your manuscript will be transformed into both a professional looking eBook and a paperback print book with custom layouts, font selections and image placement options.

In this book you will find step-by-step instructions on how to:

• Publish both your eBook and paperback using the Amazon Kindle Direct Publishing (KDP) platform and the Amazon Kindle Create tool.

• Format your text with styles and themes.

• Build a table of contents.

• Add or edit text.

• Add, delete, resize, and/or align images.

• Preview how your eBook will display on tablets, phones, and Kindle E-readers and create a file to publish to KDP.

• Automatically create a clickable table of contents for your eBook.

• Automatically create a page number table of contents for your paperback print book.

Throughout this book, I will use a real case study of my own mystery novel to demonstrate how digital publishing works in practice but there are specific sections for non-fiction books in each chapter.

Information is provided for text created using both Microsoft Word and Google Docs. Where relevant, additional information is added for text created using Apple Pages.

What I will NOT be covering?

• How to write your book, whether fiction or non-fiction.

• How to identify target markets for your book prior to writing.

• How to market and promote your published books.

• Formatting information for fixed-format eBooks which are not designed to flow and resize in electronic format. These tend to be books where the images and text have been designed to be read in specific orientations. Amazon KDP provides detailed instructions on how to turn heavily illustrated books such as graphic novels, comics, manga and children's books into Kindle books and you can find out more here: https://amzn.to/2wi5PTa.

Terminology

There is a lot of confusion about whether an electronic format of a book is an eBook, an e-book or eBook. For example, The New Oxford Dictionary for Writers and Editors [2014] uses e-book with a hyphen.

The Amazon KDP platform uses **eBook** and for simplicity and consistency, this is the format used throughout this book.

In Summary

My goal in writing this book is to provide simple, clear instructions on how to leverage the power of Kindle Direct Publishing to professionally publish your book in the format you want.

No fluff or padding. Just practical information so that you can publish your book – fast!

PART ONE. HOW TO CREATE AND PUBLISH A KINDLE EBOOK

1

STRIPPING BACK THE FORMATTING OF YOUR MANUSCRIPT

What makes electronic eBooks different from printed books?

A print book, such as one the book you are reading now, is made up of fixed and fully formatted text. During any conversion process to an EPUB or Kindle mobi electronic eBook file, your manuscript.doc(x) file will be converted into a "reflowable" responsive eBook format.

This type of file format will automatically adjust the orientation and shape of the contents according to the device your reader is using to read the text, such as tablet, computer or mobile phone, in portrait or landscape mode. Your novel will therefore be displayed correctly and fill the screen of the reader's device.

Kindle Direct Publishing (KDP) uses converter software to transform your document into a reflowable Kindle mobi format file which offers the end reader a wide range of custom options.

Kindle eBooks allow the reader to resize text and change the font on all Kindle devices and the free Kindle reading applications.

On the Kindle app on my iPad, for example, I am offered a range of eight fonts: Amazon Ember Bold, Baskerville, Bookerly, Caecilia, Georgia, Helvetica, Open Dyslexic and Palatino. Plus, I have a range of line spacing options to select from and two font size adjustment buttons. **Aa**⬇ to reduce the font size, and **Aa**⬆ to increase the size of the font. There are also four choices of background page colour.

This level of user customization means that the base coding for the eBook must be as simple and logical as possible.

Above all, your book will be standardised by the KDP converter to make sure that the reading experience for your book is consistent across the large range of reading devices and Kindle apps now available.

That's why the first part of preparing your manuscript to be published as a Kindle eBook is one of the hardest.

You know all those lovely decorative fonts, coloured text and paragraph styles which you used to make your text look appealing?

Sorry. *This is going to hurt*. They must go.

The KDP system will automatically convert your text document into one long continuous piece of computer code when it creates the Kindle mobi file. It will strip out all the unwanted formatting in order to keep the code as clean and simple as possible. This includes font families, pages numbers and headings and footers.

That's why you have to tell the system where the new chapter page breaks are and what styles you want to apply to specific parts of your document such as chapter headings and body text, before you upload your file.

The eBook editing software will then use your styles to create a stylesheet for your electronic document to make sure that all the styles are consistent for the reader.

Yes, I know that this is a completely different way of looking at your manuscript, but hopefully you can now see that eBooks are fundamentally strings of computer code and the cleaner and simpler you can make your manuscript before you upload it onto KDP, the easier it will be to convert the text into a stunning electronic eBook which will be easy for your readers to enjoy. All eBooks also go through an Amazon review process to ensure that the formatting and content meets the KDP quality standards.

The good news is that KDP system means that you don't have to know anything about coding to create a professional looking eBook and print paperback which is fully acceptable to the KDP converter programmes.

Kindle publishing works with several word processing applications, such as Microsoft Word, Apple Pages, together with Open Office Writer, Google Docs and other word processing software that export to the .doc(x) format.

Step One. Final Editing, Spelling Checks and Proofread

Now is the time to go through the final draft of your manuscript in detail before starting formatting.

Spelling mistakes, huge grammar errors and copyediting glitches, such as someone's name changing halfway through a novel, or the same paragraph being repeated several times, distract your reader and spoil their enjoyment of your work.

Even worse, they mark you out as being unprofessional and result in poor reviews.

• Have you had the book edited by someone who can be objective about the text?

• Have you read the final draft of the book out loud to yourself? This can pick up missing words, words that you have repeated several times in the same sentence and incorrect paragraph and chapter break points. It is easy to accidently delete the end of a sentence in error. Now is the time to pick these errors up.

• Have you used the automatic spelling and grammar check programs available in your word processing package?

Take the time to run a last spellcheck and proofread your document. It is so easy to miss a word that has the correct spelling but is the wrong word for that context. I know because I have done this myself many times, and I still see it in traditionally published books.

Only move onto the formatting stage when you are completely happy that you cannot improve your document further and you are totally happy to share your work with readers.

Step Two. Remove all formatting

The stylesheet for your electronic book file works using general simple styles instead of the formatting you used when you created your text document.

The simplest and fastest thing to do is to get back to the basic text, which means stripping out ALL the formatting in the entire document.

That will ensure that you are not working with a document in which you have used more than one style for the same kind of text in different parts of the book.

Create a new copy of your master text document to work on as your electronic book file. You can use your original master document to create the print format of your book.

For Word. Open your document. Press Ctrl +A to select the entire document. Click the *Clear all formatting* button in the Font header menu to remove all formatting.

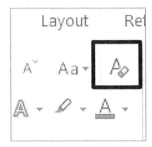

For Google Docs, press Ctrl +A to select the whole document, then go to Format and select *Clear formatting*.

Step Three. Turn off Automatic Numbering and Automatic Bullet Lists
In some languages, the dialogue in your novel is indicated with a dash instead of a quotation mark. eBook readers may change that formatting and disrupt the reading experience. This means that you should replace automatic dialogue marks with manual dash marks if you are using them to indicate where dialogue begins.

<u>Non-Fiction Authors</u>. Automatic numbered and bullet lists do not convert well into electronic documents, especially where you have a hierarchy of several bullet levels.

To create a bullet point, place your cursor at the beginning of the text, press down the Alt key and simultaneously press the number 7 on the keypad. Then insert a space before the first word of the text of that bullet point. Repeat the process for each bullet point on the list.

You can also create a bullet point by using the **Insert Symbol** tab in the top menu, then selecting a bullet symbol, such as bold circle, followed by a space before the text.

Step Four. Remove the Page Numbers and any Headers or Footers

Electronic documents don't use page numbers or header or footer text, since they are one long continuous stream of code.

For Word and Google Docs. Double click in the header or footer of your document where you have your page numbers. Delete the page number together with any text you may have in both the header and footer of your document.

Step Five. Remove the Forced Line Breaks and Paragraph Breaks

Many writers use the Enter key to add an extra line between paragraphs.

All these extra breaks need to be removed.

Don't worry – we are going to add in extra spaces between paragraphs later. But for now, they must be taken out so that all your text is spaced the same way.

To find all forced line breaks and paragraph breaks, click the Paragraph mark in the Paragraph menu. This is also known as the Pilcrow mark.

What you will now see are all the hidden paragraph breaks that you have inserted as you wrote your novel.

Now comes the difficult part.

You need to go through your document and delete any unwanted paragraph breaks or soft returns so that you only have one paragraph break at the end of each paragraph of text.

For example. Here is an unedited extract of text from the case study novel I am using for this book.

Extract from original text.

~~~~~~

Lottie peered out through the window and instantly recognized the owner of La Cucina, Elspeth Bruni, and her son Luca. She was about to ask Rosa what was happening when Luca started waving his arms about and gesturing towards a taller smartly dressed man who was standing in silence next to Elspeth.

Lottie couldn't hear exactly what they were arguing about, but whatever it was, Luca was not happy. Just as Elspeth started to move towards him, Luca pushed a bundle of loose papers at her, then turned and stomped away with a furious look on his face.

~~~~~~

Extract from original text with the paragraph (pilcrow) icon turned on.

~~~~~~

> Lottie·peered·out·through·the·window·and·instantly·recognized·the·owner·of·La·
> Cucina,·Elspeth·Bruni,·and·her·son·Luca.·She·was·about·to·ask·Rosa·what·was·
> happening·when·Luca·started·waving·his·arms·about·and·gesturing·towards·a·taller·
> smartly·dressed·man·who·was·standing·in·silence·next·to·Elspeth.¶
> ¶
> Lottie·couldn't·hear·exactly·what·they·were·arguing·about,·but·whatever·it·was,·Luca·
> was·not·happy.·Just·as·Elspeth·started·to·move·towards·him,·Luca·pushed·a·bundle·
> of·loose·papers·at·her,·then·turned·and·stomped·away·with·a·furious·look·on·his·
> face.¶
> ¶

~~~~~~

As you can see, there is an extra paragraph break at the end of each sentence which has inserted an extra line between the paragraphs. All these extra paragraph breaks must be removed.

~~~~~~

Lottie·peered·out·through·the·window·and·instantly·recognized·the·owner·of·La·
Cucina,·Elspeth·Bruni,·and·her·son·Luca.·She·was·about·to·ask·Rosa·what·was·
happening·when·Luca·started·waving·his·arms·about·and·gesturing·towards·a·taller·
smartly·dressed·man·who·was·standing·in·silence·next·to·Elspeth.¶
Lottie·couldn't·hear·exactly·what·they·were·arguing·about,·but·whatever·it·was,·Luca·
was·not·happy.·Just·as·Elspeth·started·to·move·towards·him,·Luca·pushed·a·bundle·
of·loose·papers·at·her,·then·turned·and·stomped·away·with·a·furious·look·on·his·
face.¶

~~~~~~

Scene Breaks Within a Chapter

There is one exception to this recommendation.

If you have inserted extra lines to separate out two scenes within the same chapter, you can insert one line with three asterisks as a scene separator to indicate a break in the text.

For example

~~~~~~

Lottie couldn't hear exactly what they were arguing about, but whatever it was, Luca was not happy. Just as Elspeth started to move towards him, Luca pushed a bundle of loose papers at her, then turned and stomped away with a furious look on his face.

***

Before Lottie could say anything, Rosa took hold of her arm and gestured with her head towards the other end of the kitchen.

~~~~~~

Step Six. Make sure all your chapters start on a new page

If you have been using paragraph breaks to force your new chapter to start on a new page, then the process you have gone through in step four will cause chaos when converted.

For Word and Google Docs. To make sure that each new chapter starts on a fresh page, use *the Ctrl +Enter* keys to insert a Page Break.

For Word. You can also use the *Layout* Tab in the menu, then *Breaks* then *Page* or the *Insert Page Break* function from the Pages menu in Word.

Step Seven. Remove Tabs

Many authors use tabs to indent the first word of each paragraph in the text.

All these tabs must be deleted.

Don't worry – we'll use document styles to set standard indent rules later.

Step Eight. Remove Double Spaces

It is so easy to accidently press the space bar twice and insert a double space between letters or at the end of the sentence.

Unfortunately, double spaces really confuse the eBook conversion process and can destroy the smooth reading of your novel.

To make it easier, use the *Find and Replace* tool in Word to replace all the double spaces with a single space.

Go to the Editing menu, open the Replace box, and press the Space bar twice in the *Find What* field. Then go to the *Replace* With field and press the space only once.

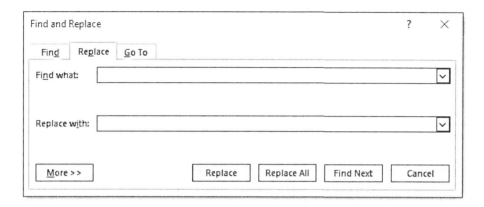

You can *Replace All* or use the *Find Next* option to see where the error has occurred and replace the double space with a single space.

Step Nine. Images

Some authors like to use an image of:

• Their publishing or author brand on the title page of their book.

• An author photo in their About the Author Page.

• Book cover images of other books which are available now or on pre-order.

The correct way to add an image to the text in the front or back matter of your novel is to use the *Insert Image* function of your word processor.

To make sure that the image stays where you want it to go, it is best to place the image *In Line With Text* which locks it on a separate line between two paragraphs or text blocks.

Then centre the image on the page. This makes the image easier to see when the eBook is being read on a small screen, for example, a smart phone.

In Word. Click on the Image then the Image Layout Options.

The *In Line with Text* options should be shaded as live.

Here is an example where I have added an image of the book cover for the next book in a cozy mystery series at the back of the book.

In Google Docs. Click on the image and make sure that the *In line* option is live.

For example: This image was also centre aligned with the text.

Important. If you have added a copy of your eBook cover to the first page of your document, you should remove this now.

The KDP system will link the eBook cover you upload into KDP with the text of your manuscript during the publishing phase. If you keep the cover image, then your reader will see two cover images which can be confusing. Best to keep to a standard text title page.

Righty. You should now have a "clean" version of your manuscript.

Time to add simple formatting instructions back in the document again so that it is ready to be uploaded onto KDP.

2

USING SIMPLE STYLES TO REBUILD THE STRUCTURE OF YOUR NOVEL OR NON-FICTION EBOOK

What do I mean by the Structure of your eBook?

If you pick up a traditionally published book, you will notice that the first page of that book is not the first page of chapter one.

Instead there is what is called **"Front Matter"** which are those pages before the text begins, then the **Main Body Text,** which is broken down into chapters and sections, and then the "**End Matter**" which is everything that comes after the main body text.

Independent publishers producing quality eBooks and print on demand paperback books should follow the same publishing rules when it comes to designing the interior layout of the manuscript of their book. The front and end matter pages do not have to be very long or complex but including these pages in any book demonstrates your professionalism.

Kindle Book "Look Inside" Feature.

Because the reader has the opportunity to read a sample of the book using the *look inside* feature on the Kindle store page for your book, many independently published authors move the copyright page and other non-essential parts of the book to the end matter.

This allows the reader browsing your book to read the Table of Contents and scan the opening pages of the body text of your book in the sample text. This could be the thrilling first page of chapter one of a novel, or the introduction to your non-fiction book where you have skilfully addressed precisely how you are going to solve a problem for the reader.

One of the many benefits of publishing your own book is that you determine precisely how you want your work to be presented and the layout of your finished book.

The interior design and layout of independently published books is not fixed and will vary from project to project depending on the content of your work.

TYPICAL PARTS OF A FICTION BOOK

The Front Matter of a Novel.

The Title Page. The title and any subtitle of your book, the name of the author and the publisher if you are using a publishing name.

Advance praise for the book and editorial reviews. (Optional)

Personal Dedication. (Optional)

About the book or note from the author. This can be useful if your book is part of a series. (Optional)

A Table of Contents. This is a requirement for Kindle eBooks.

The Body Text of a Novel. The main text is broken down into chapters.

The End Matter of a Novel.

Acknowledgements. (Optional)

A list of other books from the author. (Optional)

A note from the author which may ask the reader to leave a review. (Optional)

A link to a free reader magnet when the reader joins your email list. (Optional)

The copyright page for the book.

TYPICAL PARTS OF A NON-FICTION BOOK

The Front Matter of a Non-Fiction book.

The Title Page. The title and any subtitle of your book, the name of the author and the publisher if you are using a publishing name.

Advance praise for the book and editorial reviews. (Optional)

Personal Dedication. (Optional)

About the book or note from the author. This can be useful if your book is part of a series. (Optional)

A Preface written by a subject matter expert. (Optional)

A Table of Contents. This is a requirement for Kindle eBooks.

The Body Text of a Non-Fiction book.

An Introduction to the book.

The main text is broken down into parts, sections and chapters where necessary.

The End Matter of a Non-Fiction book.

Appendix (Optional)

Reference List (Optional)

List of Diagrams and Illustrations. (Optional)

Acknowledgements. (Optional)

A list of other books from the author.

A note from the author which may ask the reader to leave a review.

A link to a free reader magnet when the reader joins your email list. (Optional)

The copyright page for the book.

Why is it important to understand the parts of a book?

When you format your manuscript, the heading of each page in the front matter, the title of each part, section and chapter of the body text, and each page in the back matter must be given the **Heading 1 style** to be included in the automatic Table of Contents in an eBook.

The key thing to remember is – keep the format very simple and use styles to make sure that all your text is formatted the same way throughout your book.

There are two key styles which should be set:

1.Your Normal Style for the body text of your novel.

2.The Chapter Heading Style.

Step One. Set the Normal Body Text Style

If you have removed all the unwanted formatting, the text of your novel will already be set to the "Normal" style. The best way to ensure that your text reads correctly as an eBook is to modify this Normal style to create one consistent style for font, paragraph indents and line spacing.

Font and Font Size

When you upload the .doc(x) file of your book into KDP, the Amazon system will update the fonts you have used to a default standard font and font size when it creates the reflowable eBook file. This allows the reader to change the font type and the font size on the reading device that they are using to read your book.

For example. Bookerly (serif) and Ember (sans serif), both Kindle-exclusive fonts, aim to provide the same style of modern print books while providing great readability on digital screens of all sizes.

To support this conversion process, I would recommend changing the Normal font to a standard font and font size.

Fiction Authors.

I would recommend changing the Normal style of your novel to a serif font from the start which you know that KDP will accept. For most novels, readers will have a better reading experience of large amounts of text when you use a serif style font in font size 10 or 11.

Reminder. Serif fonts have small tails at the end of the letters. Non-serif fonts are cleaner and straighter in style. For example. Here are two serif fonts: Palatino and Georgia.

Non-Fiction Authors.

Most non-fiction is created using non-serif fonts for both the body text and the chapter headings. For example. Here are two non-serif fonts: Arial and Lucida Sans.

The book you are reading now was written using the Roboto non-serif font as the normal style with Bebas Neue chapter headings.

Using Bold and Italics

These can be used to add emphasis to text. Body text made up of entirely bold or italic text will be rejected.

<u>Font Colour</u>

Coloured text should also be changed back to standard black throughout the document.

How to change the Normal Style of your document.

Select a few paragraphs of text from a chapter in your novel. The style of that text will display in the Styles header bar.

In Word.

Change the font and font size of your text until you are happy with it.

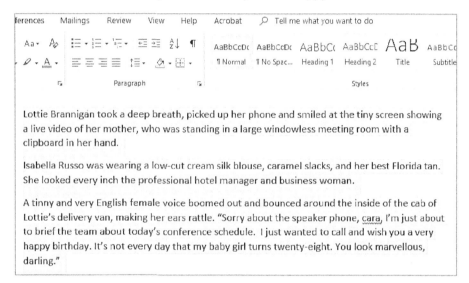

In this example I want to change the font from Calibri 11point to Georgia 11point.

Click on the *Normal* style which should be highlighted then click on *Update Normal to Match Selection*.

Your Normal style for the entire document has now been changed.

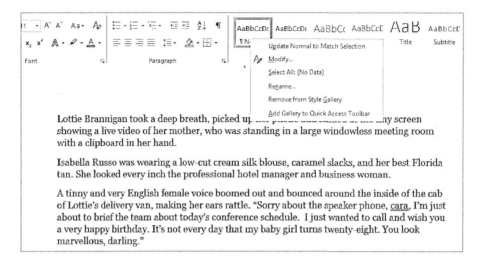

In Google Docs.

Select the text. Check that the header tells you that this is the Normal text style.

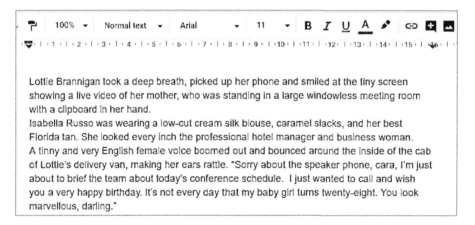

In this example the current font is Arial 11 point.

Let's change it to Georgia 11 point.

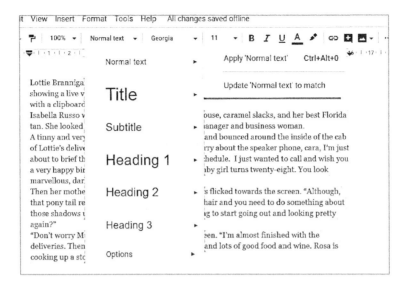

Click Update 'Normal text' to match.

Text Justification

The text in reflowable Kindle eBooks is fully justified, both right and left, by default.

You can set the layout of the body text to be fully justified using the paragraph formatting tool and the Alignment options.

Replace manual paragraph tabs with auto indents for the first line of paragraphs

Fiction Authors

Most novelists prefer to indicate a new paragraph by indenting the text on the first line of each paragraph. Instead of tabs you should use paragraph styles to set how much of an indent you want.

Using the same example of chapter text, I would suggest using a hanging indent for the first line of each paragraph of 0.3cm.

In Word.

Select a few paragraphs of body text from your novel.

Click on the Paragraph options in your header bar.

Then go to General Alignment. Use the dropdown arrow to change the Alignment from Left Aligned to Justified.

Then set the *Special First Line indentation* to 0.3cm (or the equivalent in the US) and click OK to insert the paragraph indent.

Some fiction authors prefer to use a larger first line indent of 0.4 cm so feel free to experiment with a large block of text to see how changing the first line indent impacts both the appearance and the reading experience of your novel.

See how your chapter looks and if you want a larger or smaller indent, simply repeat the process and change the width of the indent in the first line in the paragraph formatting styles.

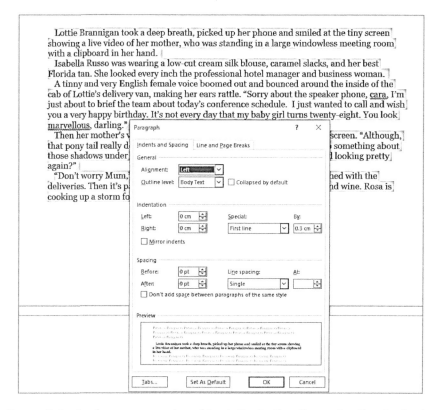

In Google Docs. Select a few paragraphs of text. Go to the *Format* option in the header bar, then *Align and Indent.*

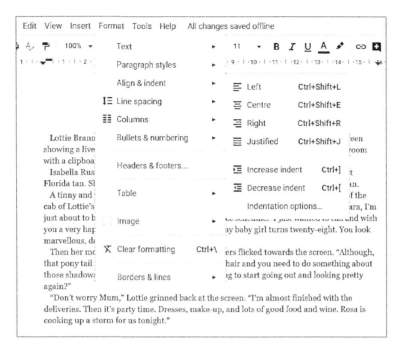

Click on the Justified option on the right sidebar.

Then select the *Indentation Options* and then *Special, First Line* and set the indent you prefer.

<u>Non-Fiction Authors</u>

By convention, non-fiction authors use block paragraphs of text with one extra line spacing to indicate the start of a new paragraph.

To create a line space after each paragraph, use the paragraph formatting option to add a space after the text.

Select a few paragraphs of body text from your book.

Click on the Paragraph options in your header bar.

Go to the Spacing option at the bottom of the pop-up and add a value to the AFTER "pt" box. The default would be a single space line, so 11point if you are using 11point text. Feel free to experiment with the gap until you have the effect that you are looking for.

At this point your normal body text should be:

• Fully justified.

• Have a standard consistent font and font size for your genre.

• Have a paragraph indent if you are using one.

• Have an extra line space after each paragraph if you are using one.

Step Two. Set the Chapter Heading Style

It is essential that you tell the Kindle KDP or Kindle Create conversion software where your chapters, sub-headings or page titles are. The system must be able to recognise the headings so that the system can create an automatic table of contents for you.

Heading 1 Style

All chapter titles and section/page headings should be marked as Header 1 style if you want them to be included in the Table of Contents of your eBook.

The easiest thing to do is to work through your text and change any heading that you wish to have in your table of contents to the Heading 1 style.

This includes the header title text of:

<u>Front Matter.</u> About the Book, Note from the Author. Dedication.

<u>Body Text.</u> Every Chapter Title.

<u>Back Matter</u>. Any Acknowledgements. Other Books by the Author. About the Author page. The Copyright page.

Heading 2 and 3 Styles

All major sub-headings within your chapters should be assigned the Heading 2 style.

All less important subheadings should be given the Heading 3 style, and so on.

<u>BOOKS DIVIDED INTO PARTS OR SECTIONS</u>

If you are creating a detailed non-fiction book, you may have to use several heading styles so that the table of contents hyperlinks to the correct page.

For example. Imagine that your non-fiction book has been divided into three parts. Inside each part are chapters. You must tell the Kindle conversion program where each part begins and where each chapter begins. In this example, I would recommend creating a new page for each new part and giving the text on that part title page the Heading 1 style. Then the heading for each chapter inside that part is given the Heading 2 style. The table of contents list will then indent these chapters inside the part description.

The process for assigning all header styles is the same.

In both Word and Google Docs, simply click at the chapter or page heading and select Heading 1 style.

For example.

In Word. The chapter one heading is currently in Normal and left aligned.

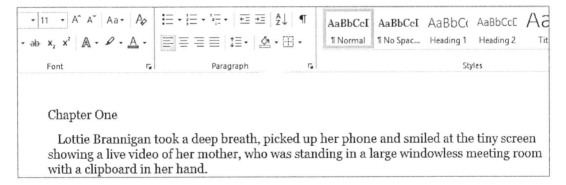

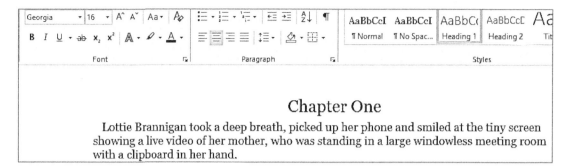

In Google docs.

Select the chapter heading. Click on the *Normal text* header and click the down arrow to *select Heading 1*, then *Apply 'Heading 1'.*

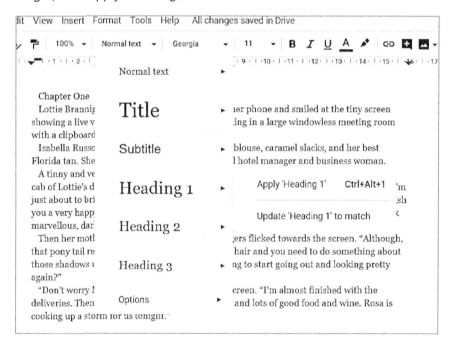

You can now update the font and font size of the chapter headings and change the alignment. For example, if you want to place your chapter heading in the centre of the page. Many authors also prefer to have a line space after the chapter heading. To do this, you can make the change in your document, select the heading text and apply the "Update Heading 1 to match" in the style menu. Or go into the style menu and change the settings for Heading 1 using the Format Font and Paragraph menus.

Now work through the document and apply the saved Heading 1 style to every chapter title and page title that you want to be included in the table of contents for your book.

Then check that any headings within the chapters have been given a Heading 2 and Heading 3 style.

Step Three. Create an Automatic Clickable/Hyperlinked Table of Contents

Once you have created Heading styles for your document, you can use the word processing software to scan your document and create a list of the headings as a Table of Contents for your document. The top level of the list will be Heading 1 followed by Heading 2 and 3 etc. but you can select how many levels you want in the Table of Contents and which Headings are to be included.

To Create the Automatic Table of Contents

The simplest and fastest way to create a Table of Contents for your eBook is to use the word processing software to generate one for you. You can be confident that the page location will always be correct and if you make changes to the text, it only takes one click to update the contents.

Put your cursor in the front matter of the document where you want to insert the table of contents, usually just before the main text. Type in the word Contents or Table of Contents and give it a Normal style – you don't usually want the Table of Contents to be in the listing.

In Word.

• Go to the References tab in the header bar.

• Click on Table of Contents.

• Then select the Custom Table of Contents option at the bottom of the box.

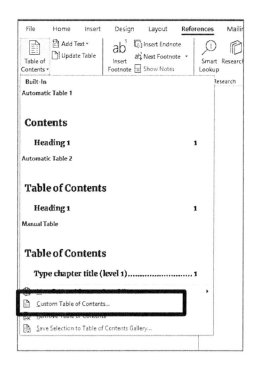

· Uncheck "Show page numbers".

· Check "Use hyperlinks instead of page numbers".

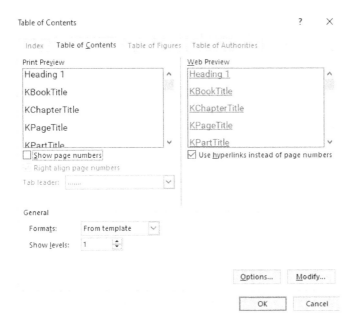

• Go to General. Show levels

> This is where you can decide how many Headings you want to display in the Table of Contents.
>
> For fiction writers, this will usually be 1 level (Heading 1) unless your novel is divided into parts, in which case change this to 2.
>
> Non-fiction books may have parts, chapter headings, section headings and subheadings, so you will need to decide on how deep you want the Table of Contents to show. 2 levels usually work well (Heading 1 and Heading 2) but this is entirely dependent on your specific book.

• Click on "Options"

> Scroll down all the styles that you can use to build a Table of Contents (TOC).
> **Select Heading 1** as TOC level 1 and put numbers against the other levels that you want to use. So, Heading 2 would be (2) and Heading 3 would be level (3) etc.

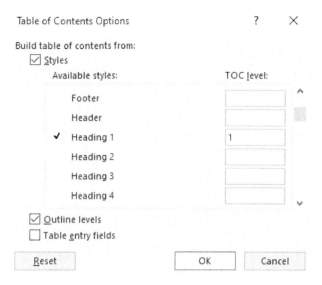

• If you only want to use Heading 1, delete the (1) number against any other style that may be listed as an option.

• Click OK. The software will now detect all of the headings that you have selected and list that text with a hyperlink associated with the position of that header text in your document.

Modifying the Table of Contents Style
In Word.

• Go to the References tab in the header bar.

• Click on Table of Contents. Then use the down arrow to select Custom Table of Contents option at the bottom of the box.

• To change the font and font size used, select the Modify Option. This will take you to the font option menu and you can select any font combination that you wish.

To update the table of contents at any time, simply click on the table and right click if you are using a mouse. Then click on Update Field.

Update Table of Contents   ?   ✕

Word is updating the table of contents. Select one
of the following options:

⦿ Update page numbers only

◯ Update entire table

          OK   Cancel

Inserting a Table of Contents in Google Docs.

• Place your cursor in the position where you want the Table of Contents.

• Go to Insert in the Editing mode, then Table of Contents.

• Select the option which will show blue bars – these will be hyperlinked locations. [Page numbers are for print books.]

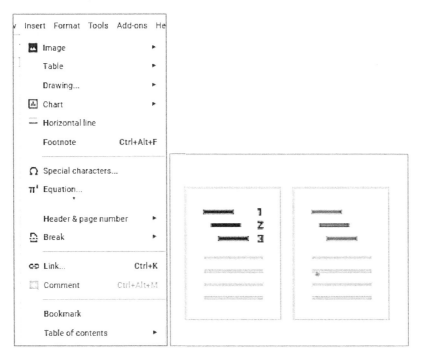

• Change the font and font size of the entries by selecting the entire table of contents then clicking on the font options in the header.

If you make changes to your document that affect the table of contents, you can update the table of contents by right clicking the table of contents and choosing **Update Field**.

This will update the hyperlinked location of the header in an electronic document.

SAVE your document as a new .docx file.

Great! Now save your formatted document as a **.docx format file** which is ready to be converted into a Kindle eBook. This is the preferred document type.

For more information go here> https://kdp.amazon.com/en_US/help/topic/G200634390

Step Four. Preview and Validate your document before uploading

The Amazon Kindle Previewer Tool

Amazon have provided an excellent free preview tool for independently published authors and I would recommend that you check your document using the Kindle Previewer before you start the publishing process inside KDP.

Kindle Previewer helps you preview and validate how your books will appear when delivered to Kindle customers before you publish.

The latest version of Kindle Previewer has the full Enhanced Typesetting features so that you can check the appearance of images, tables, font alignments, word spacing, hyphenation and text features.

Kindle Previewer is available for Windows and Mac OS X.

Download the most recent version of Kindle Previewer through the link at

https://www.amazon.com/gp/feature.html/?docId=1000765261

Take the time to scan the features of this powerful previewer tool.

One of the key benefits of Kindle Previewer is that you can see what your document will look like on any kind of reading device before you upload it onto KDP. Simply use the toggle switch under Device Type to change the device and the orientation of the device.

You can change the font, font size and navigate within your document.

This is particularly useful if you are a non-fiction writer and have included images, charts and tables in your document. Many readers prefer to read books on smart phones and tablets. This is your opportunity to see how your document will appear to readers on small, narrow screens.

To load a text document onto the Kindle Previewer:

Go to File in the top left menu bar.

Click on Open Book. This will take you to your document folders where you can find your manuscript.

It can take a few minutes for the document to be converted into a Kindle eBook and display on the previewer screen.

<u>Key Elements to check using Kindle Previewer</u>

1. The Cover pages. Does the text appear in the centre of the page? Is there a clear separation between the title and the author name? It is always useful to test this in the smart phone device option.

The text will display differently on a Kindle E-reader as opposed to the Kindle app. For example.

Device set to Phone

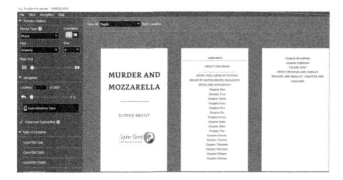

Device set to Tablet

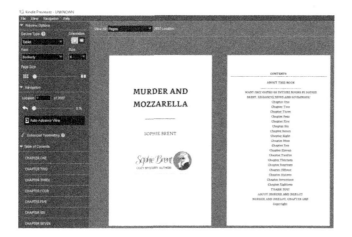

Device set to Kindle E-reader.

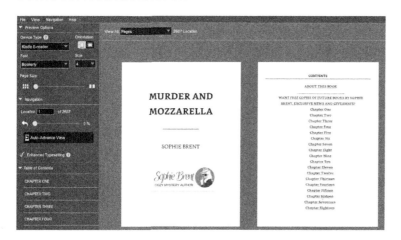

You will notice that the cover text is displaced on the Kindle E-reader and the table of contents is hyperlinked and underlined as opposed to blue hyperlinked.

2. The Hyperlinked Table of Contents is a key part of any electronic book.

Does every one of the chapter headings link through to the correct location in the document?

As an additional check toggle the Table of Contents option to open up the display.

Carefully check that every chapter heading and page heading that you want to be included in the Table of Contents is listed. If one is missing, go back to your text document, change the heading style to Heading 1 or 2 or 3 as appropriate, then save the document as a new file and upload it again into the Previewer.

3. Navigation inside the document

The aim is to simulate the same reading experience as someone buying your book.

Go to the Navigation tab in the top menu bar.

Check that each of the links takes the reader to the correct location in the book.

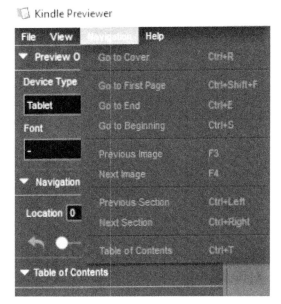

#4. The Appearance of the text

Do all the chapter headings look the same? They should do if you have used the Header 1 style. One thing to check is the spacing between the heading and the first line of text.

Body text alignment. The text should automatically be fully justified with the small indent that you created at the start of each new paragraph. Non-fiction authors should check the spacing between paragraphs does not appear too large.

Blank pages. It is very easy to accidently insert a page break and create a blank page which will confuse readers.

Scene Break Symbols. If you have used symbols to introduce a scene break [usually three asterisks] with a space above and below the symbols, check that the spacing is not too large and that the symbols are centred. These will look different according to the font the reader has selected on their device.

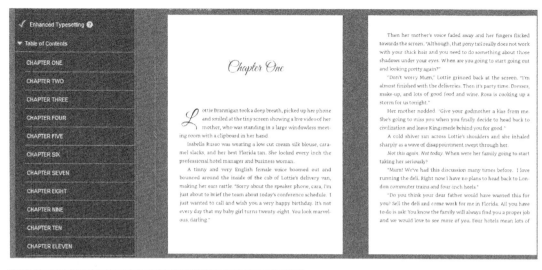

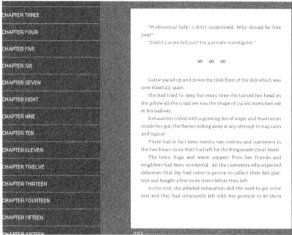

Hyperlinks in the text and Images

If you have added links in the text to, for example, your website URL or your Amazon page so that readers can review the work, check that all the hyperlinks are working.

Images should appear central and large enough to be seen but not overwhelm the page relative to the text size.

One final check. Read through your book on the screen.

It is amazing how many tiny things slip through the editing and proofreading process, no matter how many times you have read the contents.

This is your final check to make sure that the content is the best that you can make it.

In the past, I have moved chapters around in non-fiction books and changed chapter breaks in fiction books so that the text reads more smoothly.

It only takes a few minutes to update the text and reload it onto the Kindle Previewer.

This is your book! You should be proud of your work and excited to share it with readers worldwide.

Happy? Then save a new master file of your document and get ready to publish.

3

THE COPYRIGHT PAGE AND ISBN NUMBERS

The Copyright Page

After the title page in an eBook or KDP print book is a short copyright page.

For a novel, most indie authors move the copyright page to the back of the eBook so that the reader can start reading the opening scenes in the "Look Inside" sample, but for a print book it is traditionally on the reverse side of the title page.

The copyright page should have all the publishing information about the book. Including:

• The publisher's name and contact details if you have decided to create your own publisher brand for your books.

• The date of publication and the publishing history such as editions and formats.

• The copyright line. This is given as the copyright symbol, followed by the copyright holder's name and the year of first publication. For example. ©NinaHarrington.2020

• The copyright notice and assertion of rights.

• A disclaimer for fiction authors that the characters and storyline is completely imaginary.

• Credit to the cover designer or the stock photo library that was used to create the cover artwork. (Optional)

• Any catalogue details such as the British Library and the Library of Congress who hold catalogues of new books before their publication. (Print books only)

• The ISBN for that book.

Worked example of a simple copyright page for a novel.

~~~~

~~~~

What is an ISBN and do you need one?

What is an ISBN?
The International Standard Book Number is the unique identity code for your book in the world. The 13-digit number code identifies the title, edition, format, binding, release date, list price and publisher of any given format of any work in the public domain.

So ideally you should have a separate ISBN for a printed book, audiobook, graphic novel and each type of digital format: Kindle, ePUB and PDF etc.

Items that do not require ISBNs include journals, calendars, music CDs, greeting cards, individual pictures or photographs and games.

There is no legal requirement in the UK or Republic of Ireland for an ISBN, and it conveys no form of legal or copyright protection. It is used solely as a product identification number.

However, the ISBN is a compulsory sales tool if you intend to make a printed version of your book available in bookstores or public libraries, as it is the one single identifier for your book in all industry-wide book tracking and ordering systems.

Do you need an ISBN for Amazon Kindle eBooks – NO, you do not need an ISBN for an eBook.

Amazon gives each eBook a 10-digit ASIN (Amazon Standard Identification Number), which is unique to the eBook, and is an identification number for the Kindle Book on Amazon.

Do you need an ISBN for Amazon Print Paperbacks?
For Amazon Paperbacks, the answer depends on whether your distribution model.

If you plan to publish your print book as an Amazon paperback only – the answer is NO.

Amazon will provide you with a free ISBN to publish your paperback.

The publisher of the book will be listed on Amazon as "independently published". Amazon will own the ISBN for this book and be registered as the publisher, not you.

If you want Amazon to ship your printed book outside of the Amazon store in the Expanded Distribution option, then the answer is YES.

You will need an ISBN to distribute your book through the retail system outside of Amazon. The ISBN is used to order and track your book.

How do you buy an ISBN?

In the U.S.A: Bowker. http://www.isbn.org/

UK. Nielsen. http://www.isbn.nielsenbook.co.uk/controller.php?page=123

And in Australia, Thorpe-Bowker: https://www.myidentifiers.com.au/

National Library of New Zealand. http://natlib.govt.nz/forms/isn

You should allow at least 7 days for the codes to arrive in the post.

Points to consider.

• **ISBNs are not free, except in Canada,** and you may need to purchase of bundle of 10 numbers or more. So, it is always a good idea to consider how many more books you are likely to be publishing in the future before investing in a bundle of codes. For example. At the time of writing. **Bowker in the USA: 1 ISBN currently costs $125. A bundle of 10 ISBNs cost $295. Neilsen in the UK: 1 ISBN currently costs £89. A bundle of 10 ISBNs cost £159.**

• When you buy an ISBN, you are registering yourself as the publisher of your eBook. The registering body will ask for the name of the publisher for their records.

• You should carefully consider what name you are going to give to your publishing brand before you register and order the ISBNs. For example, I publish my work under the company name NinaHarringtonDigital since Nina Harrington is my brand. But I could have chosen any name I liked which was suitable for the genre and type of book I am publishing which is linked to your unique author brand. Always do an Internet search to make sure that the name you have chosen has not already been used by another author.

• **Public Legal Deposit Library Copies.** If you purchase your own ISBNs, as a registered publisher in the UK, you will be required to provide, free of charge, five copies of each printed book for the national archives. In addition, you need to supply one copy of each printed book to the British Library. These copies have to be ordered from Amazon paperbacks and posted to the libraries at your expense. Similar Legal Deposit Library schemes exist in many other countries and you will be contacted by the registration body and asked to supply free copies.

• Most readers don't even notice the name of the publisher when they buy a print book from Amazon.

• You need the ISBN to generate the barcode on your print book.

The decision is therefore a personal one and you should consider carefully whether you want your novel to be exclusive to Amazon.

Publisher Name
Many authors love the idea of having their name in their books as both the author and the owner of their own publishing brand and it can be great fun coming up with the publisher name for yourself and your books and designing a logo for the spine of your print books and the front pages of your eBook.

The publisher name you select will be published in the Product Details for your book as part of the Metadata for your Kindle eBook.

4

PUBLISH YOUR EBOOK ON KDP

Log onto your Amazon KDP account to publish your Kindle eBook.

Your Kindle Direct Publishing Account
If you don't already have a KDP account, follow the instructions on the home page to set-up your account, tax information and payment details.

For example. https://kdp.amazon.com/en_US

You will be taken to a Bookshelf page where you can **Create a New Title**.

Click on + Kindle eBook

Kindle eBook Details Page
Start working down the page, completing each section in turn until you have a complete profile for your paperback book.

• Language.

• Book Title and any Subtitle.

• Series. The Series link is particularly useful is you are considering making your novel part of a new or existing series of linked novels.

You can return to this page at any time and update the series information for the Kindle store book page for this novel.

For example. For our case study, I am publishing this cozy mystery under my pen name of Sophie Brent.

Author. Sophie Brent

Book Description

In a brick and mortar traditional bookstore you can browse the shelves which are usually organised by genre and then by the author name.

Online book distributors work in the same way – except that they are essentially huge computer databases. Books are data files which are sorted according to the information you give them about your book.

The Book Description and any Subtitle on the eBook

You have spent weeks or months writing this book and now comes the fun part – telling your ideal audience all about it!

Before you write the book details for your book and load them onto Kindle Direct Publishing and all of the other publishing platforms that you plan to use, take the time to put yourself into the position of a casual browser to the online bookstore.

I want to be enticed into reading this book by the anticipation of an inspirational and or dramatic emotional journey. The only place I will find that is from the Book Description and the Additional material the author has added about the book.

Does your book description have a compelling and irresistible hook with keywords which link to your cover image? Is the subtitle short, memorable and irresistible?

Is the book description easy to understand? Remember – this will be scanned by browsers to the online bookstore who are intrigued by the cover art.

Think about reading the description on the flap of a dust jacket or on the back cover of a printed book. How would you capture the essence of your book in a few sentences?

This will be the core information that is available for browsers scanning the digital shelves at the online bookstores.

Use the Book description and any subtitles to make the compelling short pitch.

Once your eBook is loaded onto the Kindle store you can then use the Author Central feature to add lots more information and editorial reviews for your potential readers. Make me a promise. Show me that this book will be worth my time.

You can also incorporate genre and niche keywords organically into that book description.

For example. Using the case study book. My book description reads:

> **The 1st book in the NEW Kingsmede Cozy Murder Mystery series!**
> What do you do when your elderly Italian godmother is accused of murdering the chef brought in to replace her - and she probably did it?
> *This book will delight fans of TV shows like 'Midsomer Murders' and 'Murder She Wrote' who love reading cozy mysteries such as the Agatha Raisin and Peridale Café series.*
> Lottie Brannigan thought that life was complicated enough when all she had to cope with were her friends and the latest antics of her Italian relatives, but then she finds her neighbour knocked out on his doorstep and her godmother is accused of murdering a rival chef!
> Running an Italian deli in an English country village has never been so deadly!
> **Book 1 in the Kingsmede Mystery series! A standalone witty cozy mystery with a deli owning female amateur sleuth. No cliff-hangers, swearing, intimate or graphic scenes.**

~~~~~~

You can use simple html code to add basic formatting to the book description which will appear on the book page on the Amazon Kindle store.

Don't worry, you don't need to understand computer code to do this. Just a few simple extras will help to draw a browser on the Amazon store to the parts of the book description that you feel are important.

You can always change this at any time by going back into KDP if you don't like how the book description appears on the Kindle Store.

Supported HTML for Book Description

Amazon Kindle Direct Publishing allows you to use the following html tags inside your book description area (up to date as of March 2020)

This page includes a complete list of HTML tags supported in the book description field. To avoid formatting errors, please close your HTML tags. For example, to close this tag for bold text <b>, you need to add </b>, which prevents the rest of your content from appearing as bold text.

Open HTML tag	Close HTML tag	Description
<b>	</b>	Formats enclosed text as bold
 	</br>	Creates a line break
<em>	</em>	Emphasizes the enclosed text. Generally formatted as italic.
<h4> to <h6>	</h4> to </h6>	Formats enclosed text as a section heading: <h4> (largest) through <h6> (smallest). <h1>, <h2>, and <h3> aren't supported.
<i>	</i>	Formats enclosed text as italic
<li>	</li>	Identifies an item in an ordered (numbered) or unordered (bulleted) list
<ol>	</ol>	Creates a numbered list from enclosed items, each of which is identified by a <li> tag
<ul>	</ul>	Creates a bulleted list from enclosed items, each of which is identified by a <li> tag

<p>	**</p>**	Defines a paragraph of text with the first line indented. Creates a line break at the end of the enclosed text.
<pre>	**</pre>**	Defines pre-formatted text
<u>	**</u>**	Formats enclosed text as underlined
****	****	Formats enclosed text as bold. See also <b>.
<q>	**</q>**	Encloses text in quotes.

How does this work in practice? For our example:

<h3>The 1st book in the NEW Kingsmede Cozy Murder Mystery series! </h3>

What do you do when your elderly Italian godmother is accused of murdering the chef brought in to replace her - and she probably did it?

This book will delight fans of TV shows like 'Midsomer Murders' and 'Murder She Wrote' who love reading cozy mysteries such as the Agatha Raisin and Peridale Café series.

Lottie Brannigan thought that life was complicated enough when all she had to cope with were her friends and the latest antics of her Italian relatives, but then she finds her neighbour knocked out on his doorstep and her godmother is accused of murdering a rival chef!

Running an Italian deli in an English country village has never been so deadly!

Book 1 in the Kingsmede Mystery series! A standalone witty cozy mystery with a deli owning female amateur sleuth. No cliff-hangers, swearing, intimate or graphic scenes.

You can then check what that book description looks like in text, using sites such as: https://ablurb.github.io/.

When your eBook page is live on the Kindle store, it is always a good idea to check the book description. You can edit the description at any time by coming back to this Book Details page and saving the edited version.

Keywords

You can use seven keywords or keyword phrases when you create your book details.

Your goal is to help readers to find your work in a crowded online book marketplace.

Keywords are equivalent to the words or phrases that readers can type into the Amazon bookstore search bar when they are looking for a specific type of book. They provide additional information about your book, beyond the title and subtitle of your book.

How to select the best keywords?

Think about the search terms you would use if you were looking for a book in the same genre on Amazon.

Using the mystery book as a case study: I have just searched for cozy mysteries on the Amazon.com Kindle Store and right now there are 23,475 search results across 12 categories and sub-categories, including.

Any Category. **Kindle Store.** Cozy Mystery, Cozy Culinary Mystery, Mystery Romance,. Cozy Animal Mystery, Mystery, Cozy Crafts & Hobbies Mystery, Traditional Detective Mysteries, Mystery Series, Christian Suspense, Holidays, Kindle eBooks, Kindle Short Reads.

The Amazon publishing platform will search the information you provide for your book and try and match it with the search criteria that readers are typing in.

RECOMMENDED CATEGORY LINKED KEYWORDS

If you publish on Amazon KDP you should be aware that there are certain categories where there are "keyword requirements." https://kdp.amazon.com/en_US/help/topic/G201298500

The full list is based on the standard BISAC Subject Headings used by traditional publishers which you can find here: https://bisg.org/page/bisacedition

"During title setup, you'll select a BISAC (Book Industry Standards and Communications) code. The codes you choose, along with your selected keywords, are used to place your book into certain categories, or browse paths, on Amazon. After your book has an Amazon listing, your book's category will appear under the Product Details section of your listing. This will be the path a customer can follow to find your book."

BISAC is an acronym for Book Industry Standards and Communication. This is basically "a uniform list of book categories that the whole industry agrees upon."

If Amazon KDP recommends keywords in specific categories, then this is the first place I should go to.

NOTE. There are two lists. One for Amazon.com and one for Amazon.co.uk. This is because categories may have different names on these two Kindle Stores and there can be different sub-categories.

For example. I am interested in Cozy Mystery Culinary.

Amazon.com has Mystery, Thriller and Suspense.

Amazon.co.uk has Crime, Mystery and Thriller.

"In order for a title to appear in the Mystery, Thriller, & Suspense sub-categories below, the title's search keywords must include at least one of the keywords or phrases listed next to the sub-category."

The full list for Mystery fiction is here: https://kdp.amazon.com/en_US/help/topic/G201276790

For example, taking the Amazon.com listing of keywords for **Mystery, Thriller, & Suspense.**

In order for a title to appear in the **Mystery, Thriller, & Suspense sub-categories** below, the title's search keywords must include at least one of the keywords or phrases listed next to the sub-category.

For authors in the UK: This category is known as "**Crime, Mystery, & Thriller**," and includes keywords that apply only on Amazon.co.uk.

Category	Keywords
Mystery, Thriller & Suspense Characters/Amateur Sleuth	amateur
Mystery, Thriller & Suspense Characters/British Detectives	british detective
Mystery, Thriller & Suspense Characters/FBI Agents	fbi
Mystery, Thriller & Suspense Characters/Female Protagonists	female protagonist
Mystery, Thriller & Suspense Characters/Police Officers	police
Mystery, Thriller & Suspense Characters/Private Investigators	private investigator
Mystery, Thriller & Suspense/Crime Fiction/Heist	heist, robbery, thief, theft
Mystery, Thriller & Suspense/Crime Fiction/Murder	murder
Mystery, Thriller & Suspense/Crime Fiction/Noir	noir
Mystery, Thriller & Suspense/Crime Fiction/Organized Crime	mob, mafia, organized crime, yakuza
Mystery, Thriller & Suspense/Crime Fiction/Serial Killers	serial killer
Mystery, Thriller & Suspense/Crime Fiction/Vigilante Justice	vigilante justice
Mystery, Thriller & Suspense Moods/Dark	dark
Mystery, Thriller & Suspense Moods/Disturbing	disturbing
Mystery, Thriller & Suspense Moods/Fun	fun
Mystery, Thriller & Suspense Moods/Humorous	comedy
Mystery, Thriller & Suspense Moods/Racy	racy
Mystery, Thriller & Suspense Moods/Scary	scary
Mystery, Thriller & Suspense Moods/Vengeful	vengeful
Mystery, Thriller & Suspense/Mystery/Cozy/Animals	cat, dog, horse, animal, pets
Mystery, Thriller & Suspense/Mystery/Cozy/Crafts & Hobbies	craft, hobby, knitting, quilting
Mystery, Thriller & Suspense/Mystery/Cozy/Culinary	food, cook, bake
Mystery, Thriller & Suspense Settings/Beaches	beach
Mystery, Thriller & Suspense Settings/Islands	island
Mystery, Thriller & Suspense Settings/Mountains	mountain
Mystery, Thriller & Suspense Settings/Outer Space	space
Mystery, Thriller & Suspense Settings/Small Towns	small town
Mystery, Thriller & Suspense Settings/Suburban	suburban
Mystery, Thriller & Suspense Settings/Urban	urban
Mystery, Thriller & Suspense/Suspense/Paranormal/General	paranormal
Mystery, Thriller & Suspense/Suspense/Paranormal/Psychics	psychic, telepathy
Mystery, Thriller & Suspense/Suspense/Paranormal/Vampires	vampire

Mystery, Thriller & Suspense/Suspense/Paranormal/Werewolves & Shifters	werewolf, shapeshifter
Mystery, Thriller & Suspense/Thrillers/Assassinations	assassin, hitman
Mystery, Thriller & Suspense/Thrillers/Conspiracies	conspiracy
Mystery, Thriller & Suspense/Thrillers/Financial	financial
Mystery, Thriller & Suspense/Thrillers/Pulp	pulp
Mystery, Thriller & Suspense/Thrillers/Terrorism	terrorism

UK-specific keywords:	
Crime, Thriller & Mystery / Crime Fiction / British & Irish / English	london, england, english
Crime, Thriller & Mystery / Crime Fiction / British & Irish / Irish	ireland, dublin, ira, irish
Crime, Thriller & Mystery / Crime Fiction / British & Irish / Northern Irish	northern ireland, northern irish, belfast
Crime, Thriller & Mystery / Crime Fiction / British & Irish / Scottish	scotland, scottish, edinburgh, glasgow
Crime, Thriller & Mystery / Crime Fiction / British & Irish / Welsh	wales, welsh, cardiff
Crime, Thriller & Mystery / Crime Fiction / Scandinavian	scandinavian, scandinavia, sweden, swedish, stockholm, norway, norwegian, oslo, denmark, danish, stockholm, nordic

For my <u>Culinary Cozy Mystery</u> I need to include the three keywords: Food, Cook, Bake.

Category	Keywords
Mystery, Thriller & Suspense Characters/Amateur Sleuth	amateur
Mystery, Thriller & Suspense Characters/Female Protagonists	female protagonist
Mystery, Thriller & Suspense/Crime Fiction/Murder	murder
Mystery, Thriller & Suspense/Mystery/Cozy/Culinary	food, cook, bake
Mystery, Thriller & Suspense Settings/Small Towns	small town
Mystery, Thriller & Suspense Moods/Fun	fun

Manual Search for Additional Keywords

I have just gone into the Kindle store on Amazon.com and typed the word cozy.

Amazon has instantly pre-populated a drop-down list with all of the search terms that other readers have already typed in.

Top of this list are: Cozy mysteries, Cozy mysteries free kindle books, Cozy mysteries kindle, Cozy witch mysteries free kindle books, Cozy Christmas murder, Cozy paranormal mysteries, Cozy mysteries boxed sets

When you click on any of these options, Amazon will then search the Kindle store database and match up all of the keywords you provided when you published the book to find books for this reader.

These are the precise terms and words that your ideal readers have used when they come to Amazon looking for a wonderful new book to read, so why not use some of these exact keywords and phrases as part of the 7 keywords in your book details if they are a good fit for your work?

Adding Keywords and Keyword phrases

You can use up to 7 search keywords to describe your book.

Keywords for this book could include, for example: cozy culinary mystery, cozy craft and hobbies, british humour and satire, women sleuths, new cozy mystery series, murder mystery and cozy mysteries kindle, so there is a wide range of options available.

How can we use keywords to make our books stand out so that readers can find them?

Our goal is to find some way of bringing our books to the attention of readers and rank our work higher in the search engine than other books.

The more keywords you have that match – the more likely it is that your book will pop up in the results page.

There are four places where you can place keywords to make your book easy to find for your ideal reader.

The Title of the book. [Murder and Merlot]

The Subtitle. This is why so many eBooks have keyword rich subtitles which seem unnecessary but are essential to help readers find your book – but don't go over the top and have huge long lists of words. [Kingsmede Cozy Mystery Book 2.]

The Book Description. Your aim should be to incorporate as many keywords as possible into the book description but make it feel natural and easy to read.

For example.

> Murder and Merlot **[A Kingsmede Cozy Mystery]**
>
> Book 2 in the NEW Kingsmede Cozy Murder Mystery series!
>
> "This book will delight fans of TV shows like 'Midsomer Murders' and 'Murder She Wrote' who love reading cozy mysteries such as the Agatha Raisin and Peridale Café series."
>
> The annual Kingsmede Wine Festival is a major event in the local calendar. No one is looking forward to it more than Lottie Brannigan. This is the perfect opportunity for her to promote the delicious food she serves at the Italian deli she inherited from her late father.
>
> But when the winning wine maker dies after eating her canapes, Lottie gets the blame for the death. Suddenly the future of her deli takes second place to a murder investigation.
>
> Book 2 in the Kingsmede Cozy Mystery series!
>
> A standalone witty cozy mystery in an English country village with a deli owning female amateur sleuth. No cliff-hangers, swearing, intimate or graphic scenes.

"*Amazon Kindle SEO is all about ranking your book higher than other books for your keywords.*" Tom Morkes

The Next Entry on the Books Details Page is Categories.

Categories are crucial. You probably already know the general category for your book. You know it's fiction, or non-fiction. You know it's romance or crime fiction, or maybe it's self-help? These are the very general classifications that high street bookstores use.

One of the benefits of digital publishing is that Amazon and other online publishing platforms have created virtual bookstore shelves with main categories, sub-categories and sub-sub-categories where readers can browse and find the precise book that they are looking for.

Digital publishing makes "niche" publishing viable again.

Assigning Categories for eBooks and Print Books

The first thing to recognise is that "Amazon is less of a store and more of a search engine." (Penny Sansevieri, 2015)

Make your book more discoverable for readers by placing it in the categories that match it best.

You are allowed to use two categories for each book.

I think of categories as virtual bookshelves on the Amazon store.

Now you need to tell Amazon which shelf your book belongs on.

The easiest thing to do is to research books on the Amazon Kindle store which are the closest match to your book and use the same two categories if you can.

Note. Your local Kindle store may not use the same categories as the USA category selection, so research your local Amazon store to ensure that you have the best category fit.

Each of these Major Categories expands down into many subcategories which may further expand into sub-subcategory and more niche categories.

For example. Here in the UK, if I expand the + on the Fiction tab I have the choice of:

General, Action & Adventure, +African American, Alternative History, Amish & Mennonite, Anthologies, Asian American, Biographical, Black Humour, +Christian, Classics, Coming of Age, Contemporary Women, Crime, Cultural Heritage, Dystopian, Erotica, Fairy Tales, Folk Tales, Legends & Mythology, Family Life, +Fantasy, Gay, Ghost, Gothic, Hispanic & Latino, Historical, Holidays, Horror, Humorous, Jewish, Legal, Lesbian, Literary, Magical Realism, Mashups, Media Tie-In, Medical, +Mystery & Detective, Native American & Aboriginal, Noir, Occult & Supernatural, Political, Psychological, Religious, +Romance, Sagas, Satire, +Science Fiction, Sea Stories, Short Stories, Sports, Superheroes, +Thrillers, Urban, Visionary & Metaphysical, War & Military, Westerns, +Yaoi Light Novels

In addition, most large categories have subcategories and even sub-subcategories. These are indicated by a + sign next to the category.

For example. The Mystery and Detective and Romance categories have additional subcategories where you can place your book.

Mystery & Detective Category. General, Collections & Anthologies, Cozy, Hard-Boiled, Historical, International Mystery & Crime, Police Procedural, Private Investigators, Traditional British, Women Sleuths.

Since I live in the UK, I have different category name options compared to the US Kindle Store.

My main category tree for this book on Amazon UK will be:

Fiction> Mystery and Detective > Cozy and

Fiction> Mystery and Detective > Women Sleuths

But I will be using keywords to indicate to Amazon.com that the US main category tree should be Fiction> Mystery and Detective > Cozy> Culinary

Yes, there is a lot of overlap from the keyword section, but this combination of the keywords you used in your book title and subtitle, your selection of seven keywords and phrases and these two categories can make all the difference in eBook marketing and promotion.

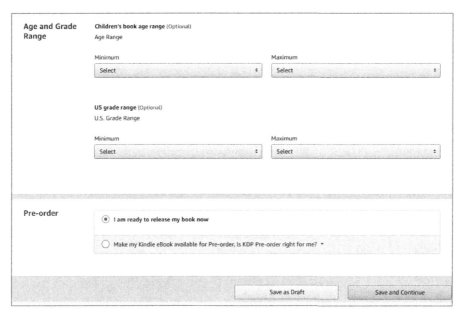

Once you have selected your two categories, move to the next entry on the Book Details page and complete the **AGE AND GRADE RANGE** section if you have written a children's book.

PRE-ORDER DETAILS

Decide whether you want to release your book now or make it available for pre-order.

Pre-order lets you offer customers the option to pre-order your book as much as 90 days before the release date. On your book's release date, customers who pre-ordered your book will automatically have it delivered to their Kindle.

There are some benefits of placing your book on Pre-Order. For example.

• If are promoting a book which has not yet been published, you can **give readers the link to the URL of the Amazon book page** so that they can read more about your new book and place an order.

• If you are on **Author Central**, you can add more detailed information, any editorial reviews, testimonials and advance review comments about the book which will be posted on the book description page. These will be in addition to the book reviews from buyers and help to add social proof and reassurance to browsers on the Kindle store.

• If you are planning to create a paperback print format of your book, you can ensure that both the Kindle and paperback formats are synced and listed on your book description page.

• It gives you time to optimise the book description page prior to the book going live.

• If you are sending out advance reader copies in exchange for an honest review, you can give your reviewers the link to the page so that they can leave a review on launch week.

• **The Hot New Releases Chart.** If anyone buys a copy of the book when it is in pre-order on Amazon, the sale is recorded on that day, which means that it kicks off the Amazon algorithm. The boost pre-launch can kick the book into the Hot New Releases Chart for that niche sub-category. Your book will be given an Amazon rank, even before it is released.

• If are planning to write, or have written, a linked series of book, you can add the link to the unpublished next book in the series at the book of your current book.

Pre-orders can therefore be part of an effective marketing campaign, especially if you have an email list.

There are three things to watch out for with the Pre-Order System

Submission Timelines
At this point in the publishing process it is possible to upload a draft version of your manuscript, then complete the final changes to your text and load the final finished version of the text during the time window before the book is released as a pre-order.

Many authors do not notice that there is an official **submission deadline**, when the document you have loaded will be locked and moved into the Amazon quality review process before going on sale.

The system will give you regular updates telling you how long you have before the submission deadline, but this is a fixed cut-off point and you will be blocked from uploading any new version of your text on or after this date.

I would recommend that you must be ready to upload a final master copy of your formatted manuscript at least a week before the pre-order release date.

If you miss the submission date, your customers/readers will be sent the draft version of your book they ordered when they placed the pre-order, complete with all of the mistakes and notes and errors that you had planned to change in the final version.

Yes, you can upload a new copy of the book as soon as the book goes live, but what would you think if you have purchased a book which is full of errors and typos?

If your miss your pre-order window and a rough draft goes live, readers might leave negative reviews that will impact sales later. So always load a publication ready draft if you can.

Sales Ranking

My process is that I don't promote or share the link to the pre-order book until I start the pre-launch campaign. The goal is to focus sales in a short time period just before and just after launch – maximising the sales ranking.

That's why I recommend scheduling the pre-order date no more than two weeks before the target launch date.

If you are looking for that magical 'bestseller' sticker, you won't get it if all your pals ordered the book during pre-order.

Reviews

Keep in mind that if you have sent advanced reading copies of your book to reviewers, these readers can't review a pre-order book on Amazon, so if you're looking to get some early reviews for it, you may want to consider directing readers to Goodreads where you can leave reviews for pre-order books.

If you are ready to release your eBook now, then your text will be complete and ready to publish.

Be sure to click *Save as Draft* or *Save and Continue* before leaving this page.

Now it's time to load your book file.

Kindle eBook Content Page

Here is where you combine your manuscript .doc(x) file and your Jpeg eBook cover to create your Kindle eBook.

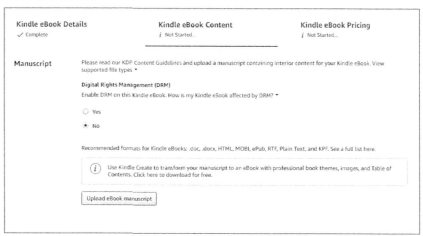

Manuscript Section.

• Click on Upload eBook Manuscript.

• Select the master document for your work on your computer. Wait to make sure that the file uploaded successfully before going to the next step and loading the Jpeg image of your eBook cover.

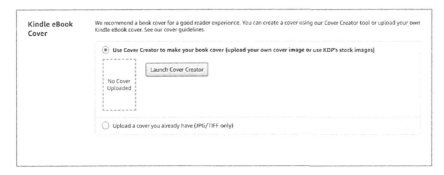

The Kindle eBook Cover

https://kdp.amazon.com/en_US/help/topic/G200645690

How to Grab the Reader with a superb Cover Design

Investing time and money in a great cover design is one of the best things you can do to market your book, no matter what genre it fits into.

We don't judge a book by its cover? *Oh yes we do.*

When we browse through the titles on Amazon or other bookseller shelves, what is the first thing we look at?

Readers can take one look at a book cover and instantly recognise all the subtle signs that tell them whether your book is something they will risk their money on, or not.

Online sites will display a small thumbnail image of your book cover, and you only have a few seconds to attract a browser before they move onto the next title on the list.

That is why it is essential that you invest in great cover design for your book. Without a quality cover, readers may not click on your book and read the book description.

Cover design for fiction is a very demanding skill. On one flat image you have to capture subtle aspects of the genre and subgenre of the book, the style of the writing and the entire mood of the novel. This is a complex combination of graphic design, styling and meticulous use of colour.

Example. Here is the cover of one of my contemporary romance titles for the Harlequin Mills and Boon RIVA and Modern Tempted line called '*My Greek Island Fling'*.

The colour range is all summer blue skies and sandy yellows with fluffy white clouds and pop splashes of pinks. My serif author name font matches the tone of the lowercase tag line at the base, and the pen and ink drawing captures a holiday romance tone.

I think it is clear to any reader, from the cover image alone, this is a fun light romance – and this is echoed in the tag line at the bottom.

Now contrast this with the draft cover idea for my cozy mystery, *Murder and Merlot*.

Note the hard, straight vertical lines of the non-serif font used for the title and author name which are all in capitals. The artwork is a high definition stock photo with a bright background colour.

That is why it is crucial that you have collected several examples of book covers from your book genre that you really like, and which would clearly signal to any reader what type of content is inside that book, before they even read the book description.

What are your options when it comes to cover design?

Option 1. Design it Yourself
Some writers are able to create an excellent design on their home computer, and there are templates available on the internet and on YouTube which describe how to use Microsoft Word, PowerPoint, Canva, Keynote, GIMP, Photoshop or similar graphic design software packages to create a very effective cover.

It is worthwhile spending a couple of hours using the search engines of the big stock image catalogues such as Shutterstock and iStockPhoto until you have a few good examples of images that you would love to be on your cover (or use a free trial if you can) and download a test image.

Then add layers and text to that photo image or images using the free software such as Canva.com, which is very easy to use and has templates for Kindle eBook covers.

Don't buy the image until you have tested it with a cover design and have fun!

I used Canva.com, to create the book cover for *Murder and Merlot*. I researched similar books on Amazon and sketched out an idea of what I wanted the cover to do.

• Clearly state that this was a cozy mystery.

• Have Murder in the title, since that was the common link to the series.

• Be attractive and bright with a large font.

• Show a village scene as the background.

Yes, it did take several days to find an image I liked and experiment with fonts and icons etc. to come up with a design which fitted my genre, but I enjoyed the process and learnt a lot.

Option 2. Purchase a Pre-Made cover
Many professional cover design companies have pre-made quality covers at reduced prices which could be perfect for your eBook. An internet search for pre-made book covers for your genre will give you an up to date list of options. E.g. The Book Cover Designer has a catalogue of designs for writers in most fiction sub-genres.

One note – think series. Does this design work as a base for more books in a similar style?

Option 3. Hire a freelance designer to create a custom cover.
One of the best sources is fiverr where you can hire a freelance from anywhere in the world for 5 to 20 US dollars to design a cover for you. Of course, you should see examples but you only pay for the work when you are completely happy with it.

Option 4. Commission a Design Company
It can pay to commission a professional cover design which is perfect for your work. The designer will need to be briefed on essential information and will usually ask for:

Examples of your favourite book covers in your subgenre. Help your designer to understand the subtle nuances of the book covers in your niche.

The type of image which you want to be on your cover. Don't buy them! The designer will be able to buy the image or a similar one cheaper and then charge you for the licence.

A quick internet search came up with Kim Killion, Damonza, Reedsy and 99Designs but there are hundreds of other eBook cover designers with a wide range of prices.

Note – I am only talking about the front cover of an eBook here. If you want to self-publish a print on demand book, then you will also need a spine and back cover design which adds to the cost, but you can find pre-made designs and templates for print books.

Key Point –Don't sabotage your hard work with a poor cover which any reader will recognise as DIY and shoddy.

Amazon Specifications for your eBook cover art

The ideal size of your eBook cover art is a height/width ratio of 1.6:1. To ensure the best quality for your image, particularly on high definition devices, the ideal dimensions for cover files are 2,560 x 1,600 pixels.

Resolution. For the best results, images should have a minimum resolution of 300 PPI (pixels per inch).

Colour. Product images display on the Amazon website using the RGB (red, green, blue) colour mode. When saving your cover image file, save your file as RGB (not CMYK or sRGB) for the colour profile.

When you are happy with your cover design and have checked that it meets all of the specifications, create a Jpeg file of your final eBook design.

Upload your Jpeg eBook cover image file.

Wait to make sure that the image uploaded successfully, and you can see a thumbnail image of the book cover.

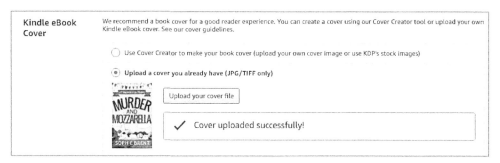

Kindle eBook Preview

This is essential! It takes a few minutes for the KDP system to check your file, convert it into a mobi file and link the book cover image with it.

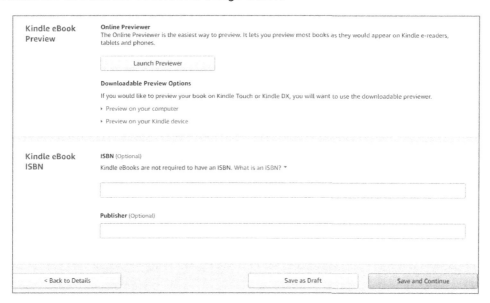

Launch Previewer when the system has completed the checks to make sure that the eBook looks the way you want it. Again, you can select whether to preview your file on a tablet or phone or Kindle E-Reader.

For example.

Scroll through the pages and check that everything has uploaded correctly.

I always check that the table of contents is working correctly and that the front and back matter have formatted correctly.

Images can be problematic and look different in the KDP previewer than on the Kindle eBook readers, so this is a good place to check that the alignment and size have carried over.

If you have added any hyperlinks to, for example, your author website, click on the link from inside the previewer.

Remember – this is your book and you can change anything you don't like at any time and reload the file onto KDP.

When you are happy with the appearance of your eBook, **click Save as Draft or Save and Continue** if you ready to move onto the next page. **Kindle eBook Pricing**

Kindle eBook ISBN

If you plan to publish your eBook exclusively on Amazon, an ISBN is not required.

Please refer back to chapter three for more information about the ISBN system and whether you need to consider having a Publisher name.

Congratulations! You have now uploaded your Kindle eBook details and the Kindle eBook Content.

Kindle eBook Pricing Page

- KDP Select Enrolment
- Territories
- Royalty and Pricing
- Matchbook
- Book Lending

Kindle Select

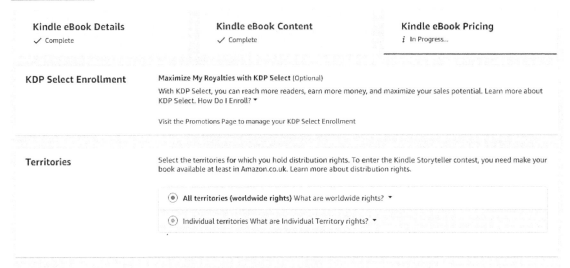

The Benefits of Enrolling in Kindle Select

Your book will be shared with readers through the Kindle Unlimited and the Kindle Owners' Lending Library, as well as on Amazon Kindle stores.

Kindle Unlimited is a subscription service for readers where they pay one monthly fee and they can download as many eBooks as they want.

The Kindle Owners' Lending Library is a collection of books that Amazon curates. Amazon Prime members who own a Kindle can choose one book from the library each month with no due dates.

Effectively you are expanding your audience and readership by enrolling your book in Kindle Select. These readers will not buy your book. Genre fiction fans, such as cozy mystery and romance readers, are prolific consumers of eBooks, and programs like Kindle Unlimited give them access to as many books as they want.

Extra Payments

The reader does not buy your book, so you are not paid the purchase or download price. Instead, every time a reader actively reads a page in one of your books, you get paid a share of a KDP Select Global Fund. You are paid by the total number of pages read in any given month. Currently this is about 0.5 cents US a page, but this can change monthly.

Each author receives a portion of the Global Fund proportional to how many pages of their titles were read. The more pages read the larger the payment.

Hence the popularity of Boxed Sets of books. More pages =more Kindle Select payments.

Special Kindle Select Promotional Opportunities

There are two extra promotional tools which are only available for eBooks enrolled in Kindle Select:

Kindle Countdown Deals, which are time-bound promotional discounting for your book while earning royalties at list price, and

Free Book Promotion where you can offer your book for free for up to 5 days out of each 90-day KDP Select enrolment period. Because your book is available for free during a free book promotion, you won't receive royalties for it while the promotion runs. You can run all 5 days at once, go one day at a time, or offer your book free for multiple days in a row. This can be particularly useful at a 'soft launch' of your book where you want readers to download a free review copy.

The Main Disadvantage of enrolling in Kindle Select

You must agree to publish that eBook exclusively with Amazon for a period of 90 days. You cannot therefore make the eBook available on other digital publishing platforms like Kobo, Apple, Barnes and Noble, Google Play etc. But you can distribute the printed format of your book to other print on demand platforms.

This is the big challenge.

There are fiction, and non-fiction, readers who do not want to read a Kindle book and prefer to read on their Kobo E-reader or buy their book on Apple iBooks or other alternatives.

Some authors feel uncomfortable putting all their eggs in one basket and ignoring the opportunities to expand their audience outside of Amazon. So, this has to be your choice.

Conclusions?

For me it comes down to one word: **Discoverability.**

Where are my readers most likely to go to find new books to read in a particular niche?

For me, the answer is Amazon, which is now one of the largest product search engines in the world.

I want and need to get my book in front of readers and help them to know that it exists. They may not be familiar with my other work. It is all down to organic searches and using search engines such as Amazon to make my book cover and title pop up.

Kindle eBook Royalties and Pricing

Be Strategic when it come to the Price of your book
Many independent authors tend to focus on the number of copies they sell and the corresponding sales rank of their books. This is totally fine, but don't forget that author income is a function of three major variables: The number of copies sold × book price × royalty rate.

As a self-publishing author, you are fully in control of the list prices for your books, and can lower the price during promotions, just like a major publishing company would do.

Royalty Rate
Click on the "Rights & Pricing" heading and scroll down to "Choose Your Royalty" and then select your preferred royalty option (35% or 70%) and your list price.

The royalty rate with Amazon KDP is set to a maximum of 70% for titles between $2.99 and $9.99 and 35% outside this range.

To qualify for the 70% royalty option, books must meet these requirements:

• The list price for the eBook must be at least 20% below the list price on Amazon for the paperback book.

• The book must be made available for sale in all geographies for which the author or publisher has rights.

• Titles must also be enrolled in KDP Select to be eligible for 70% royalty on sales to customers in Brazil, Japan, Mexico, and India.

Check the list price requirements by royalty option on the List Price Requirements page then Set Your List Price

When you set the U.S. list price for your book, Amazon will automatically convert your U.S. Dollar list price to their standard currencies in 12 other marketplaces, including British Pounds (GBP), Euros (EUR), Japanese Yen (JPY), Brazilian Real (BRL), Canadian Dollar (CAD), Indian Rupees (INR), Mexican Pesos (MXN), or Australian Dollars (AUD).

Or you can enter a specific amount by marketplace and available currency.

For example. If I select the 70% Royalty Plan and set a US price of $2.99 on Amazon.com. I can see an instant calculation of the royalty payment I can expect in each market.

I could change the UK price to, for example, £2.49 and retain all of the other prices.

Ask Yourself Four Key Questions Before You Set the List Price for your book

Who is my target audience?

Genre fiction readers demand very competitive prices for their fiction and you have to recognise that. Romance Kindle eBooks, for example, have the lowest average price in the US Kindle store, although this varies from niche to niche. Non-fiction eBooks are priced much higher and are often double the price of fiction eBooks.

<u>What is the value of my book and how is it positioned?</u>
This question refers to the book itself and to the whole positioning of your author brand. For example:

• Does your book cover a popular and relevant non-fiction topic which fits into the current zeitgeist in your niche market?

• Is your book a debut 20,000-word novella or a boxed set from a super-popular ten-part series of commercial fiction novels?

• Do you have a tribe of devoted followers and an established off-line author brand and large social media following and email list who cannot wait to read the next volume in your bestselling series?

<u>What is the price range of similar books in your category on the Amazon store?</u>
Review the other eBooks of the same length which will be on the shelf next to yours in the same category and sub-category, so that you know exactly what you are competing against on price.

<u>Research the Market</u>
Research the top 100 titles in the bestseller chart for your category and niche market to get a feel for how your eBook should be priced.

The easiest way to do this is simply write down the number of pages and the price for the top 100 titles in your chosen niche or niches on an Excel spreadsheet or GoogleSheets. Calculate the average list price and page length and note down the range of results. This should give you a good idea of how your book will fit into the current market in your niche.

Price your work within a price band which is realistic for the genre of eBook you are selling.

Think about how much you would pay as a reader, and the list price for other books of the same length and genre.

For example. Would you expect to pay the same amount for:

A 20,000-word novella or perhaps 50 equivalent pages.

A 50,000-word, 200 equivalent page category romance? And

The latest full length, 450 equivalent page blockbuster crime book from a well-known author.

I wouldn't. And yet if you look at any online bookseller you will see authors who have set a list price for their novella or short story collection which is the same as a new release of the eBook version of a bestselling novel in the charts. On the other hand, do not undervalue your work.

Take a look at your eBook reader or Kindle app. How many books do you have on it which you know that you are never going to read, or read again? Why do you want to add more? Any new eBook has to earn its place.

I think the tide has turned and many readers are now slowly turning away from free or very low-price books which they know that they will probably never read.

But it is more than that. We all lead such hectic lives with very little leisure time. If a reader is going to invest several hours of their life reading your eBook then they want to make sure that the time will not be wasted, irrespective of how little it costs.

The pressure is on authors to price our books in a way that helps readers to discover our work, and then delight them by over delivering with a compelling, well-written book which is free from errors and the best work that we can create.

That is the way to create a good reader experience and have them coming back for more.

<u>Does your book contain a lot of images of other graphic design details so that the file size is larger than 3MB?</u>
Amazon charges "delivery costs" for large files. If you select the 70% royalty option, your royalty will be 70% of your list price without VAT, less delivery costs (average delivery costs are $0.06 per unit sold and vary by file size). There are no delivery costs if you select the 35% Royalty Rate.

Delivery Costs are equal to the number of megabytes Amazon determine your Digital Book file contains, multiplied by the Delivery Cost rate.

The full cost of delivery will be displayed on the royalty calculation chart for your book, but these costs can eat into the profit margin for low price books.

For example. For Amazon.com the delivery cost is US $0.15/MB. Amazon.ca is CAD $0.15/MB. Amazon.co.uk is UK £0.10/MB

Complete each section in turn and then the magic button '*Publish Your Kindle eBook.*'

Terms & Conditions	It can take up to 72 hours for your title to be available for purchase on Amazon.
	By clicking Publish below, I confirm that I have all rights necessary to make the content I am uploading available for marketing, distribution and sale in each territory I have indicated above, and that I am in compliance with the KDP Terms and Conditions.

< Back to Content		Save as Draft	Publish Your Kindle eBook

To submit your changes and book for publishing, read through the KDP Terms and Conditions agreement, then click "**Publish Your Kindle eBook.**"

Your eBook will now go into a quality review stage.

It can take up to 72 hours for your eBook to go live on the Kindle store, but you will receive an email when it is available for purchase.

As soon as you have received the email, follow the link inside KDP for the book page for your book on the Kindle store and check that the book description reads well, and your novel has been allocated to the categories that you specified.

It may take another 24 hours before the "look inside" feature is live for your book.

Always check that the opening pages in the sample look professional and attractive. A reader coming to the Kindle store may take the time to browse your book cover and book description so make the sample pages seal the deal and persuade them to buy the book.

You can edit the book description text and any of the book details from the Bookshelf in KDP.

Congratulations! You have just published your book as a Kindle eBook!

You can now claim your eBook on your Amazon Author Central Account and start your book launch marketing activities.

PART TWO. HOW TO FORMAT AND PUBLISH PRINT BOOKS USING KDP PRINT

5

INTRODUCTION TO KDP PRINT PAPERBACKS

Since CreateSpace was incorporated into Amazon Kindle Direct Publishing (KDP) in 2018, Amazon have worked to make the system as streamlined as possible for independent authors to publish their work online in paperback format.

Every independently published author should consider leveraging the power of the Amazon KDP platform to share their work worldwide and generate real passive income.

This section gives you a complete step by step guide on how to transform your text document into a professional paperback book and then how to publish it with KDP Print.

A short mystery novel is used as a case study to show you exactly what each step looks like in practice, but the guide can be applied to both fiction and non-fiction books.

Examples will be given for documents created using both MS Word and Google Documents where possible.

Why format your print book yourself for Amazon KDP print?

• You save time and money. No need to hire a freelancer or design company.

• You can change any aspect of the book and have it available on Amazon within hours. No waiting for someone else to find the time to make the edits.

• Having the paperback format of your Kindle eBook available is a great option for those readers who prefer physical print books.

• Formatting a print book is an excellent learning experience into how print books are constructed that you can apply to any document formatting process.

• You can construct a template paperback document which you can use for any future print books.

• You have total control over how the interior design of your book will appear, including the print size, font combinations and layout. Images, graphics, quotations and poetry can be added with one click.

Most fiction authors work on the final draft of their novel in a basic word processor software such as Google Docs. or MS Word, which is great for editing and structuring the text. But when it comes to creating a professional looking print book, you need to think about how you can create and deliver the best reading experience for your reader.

Readers have an expectation that the book that they have purchased will look stunning as well as being easy to hold and read. They are investing their hard-earned money in a print book and it is your responsibility as a publisher to deliver a professional looking paperback, whether it is print on demand through a company such as Amazon KDP Print or a traditionally published print book that you would find in any bookstore.

Consideration needs to be given to elements such as font size, text style, chapter breaks, line spacing, the table of contents, copyright page, etc., and it's important that these are designed to work together in a consistent professional style, delivering an effortless read.

The last thing you want to have is a reader who leaves a one-star book review because they were disappointed about printing problems that distracted them from your novel.

As a bonus, once you have formatted your print paperback, you will have built a working template document that you can use for more books in the future. This is particularly useful if you are planning to write a series of books in a similar format.

Amazon KDP print has created an easy to use platform which makes it possible for any indie author to publish their novel as a printed paperback around the world.

This guide will show you precisely how to do that!

6

STRIPPING BACK THE FORMATTING OF YOUR MANUSCRIPT

As a reader, I know how frustrating it can be to be pulled out of a book by distractions such as a spelling mistake or breaks in the text or a sudden change in font or font size.

Consistency is crucial! The simplest and fastest way to make sure that your book, whether it is fiction or non-fiction, reads the same way in every chapter is to get back to the basic text, which means stripping out ALL the formatting in the entire document.

Then you can rebuild the document from scratch using standard styles and formatting.

Stripping out the formatting of your manuscript

Start by saving a new copy of your master text document to work on as your print format file.

If you have already created a Kindle eBook format of your book, you should already have a "clean" version of your text document.

If you are not planning to create an electronic version of your book, follow the same instructions in chapters one and two of this book to remove all of the unnecessary formatting and rebuild a simple layout for your work.

7

REBUILDING THE STRUCTURE OF YOUR PRINT BOOK

Now it is time to get creative and finalise the interior design of your paperback book.

Print paperback books do not have the same constraints as Kindle electronic books where the text must be reflowable to adapt to the end user's reading device.

Text layout and design.

There are hundreds of fonts to choose from, both free and paid, serif and non-serif.

How do you select a font? The rule is simple. Go with the font and text alignment that will deliver the best reading experience for your book, whether fiction and non-fiction.

Fiction authors, for example, tend to prefer to use serif fonts with left aligned text which is ideal for reading large blocks of text.

Non-fiction authors have the freedom to express their work to match the content of the book that will meet the expectations and needs of their ideal reader. You can use serif and non-serif fonts and text layouts that fit the content and the way you want that content to be expressed. This is one of the key benefits of independently publishing your print book – you get to choose precisely how you want your book to appear.

Images and Graphic Design. Book interior designers can create stunning layouts for paperback books. Take the time at this point to work on your ideas for the interior design of the content of your manuscript so that you are ready to format your work into a paperback print book.

Research similar books in your genre. What specific elements or layouts would you like to model in your book? Your final design will be saved as a print-quality PDF so you can be sure that your readers will receive precisely the design that you have created for your work.

8

SET THE TRIM/ PAGE SIZE OF YOUR FINISHED BOOK

The term "trim size" is used by publishing companies to describe the finished width and height of your printed book. Stacks of printed and collated papers are "trimmed" to specified dimensions after the book has been bound.

How to Determine the Ideal Trim Size for your Book
There are five factors which determine the ideal trim size.

1. The page count of your book.

2. The spine width.

3. Printing costs.

4. Your genre or niche – and hence marketability.

5. The ideal reading experience you want for your reader.

1. The Page Count

Imagine that you wish to publish a print format version of your short novel or non-fiction guide which has around 50,000 words.

The number of pages in your manuscript will depend on the font you used and the size of that font, but let's say that you have 250 words per page of text.

Your complete manuscript of 50,000 words will therefore be around 200 single sided pages at 250 words per page, or 100 double-sided printed pages, on A4 sized paper which is 8.27 inches x 11.69 inches (abbreviated to 8.27 "x 11.69") or US letter (8.5" x 11.0").

But what happens when you reduce the paper layout dimensions of that manuscript down to 5 inches wide x 8 inches tall (5" x 8"), but keep the font and content the same? The number of pages in that document will increase for the same wordcount.

The smaller the size of the paper layout, the greater the number of pages you create for the same wordcount.

The page count therefore impacts all aspects of the printing and book design process.

2. The Spine Width

There should be enough space on the spine to print the book title and author name in a legible size font. Books without spine text are considered to be pamphlets.

This is a crucial factor to understand, because **the number of printed pages in your paperback will determine the thickness of the spine of your final book.**

The more pages in your book, the thicker the spine will be, and the wider the book will appear on a bookshelf. As a general rule, you should have at least 100 to 120 double-sided printed sheets of paper to create a spine for your printed book in KDP print.

If the spine is too small to print on, then you may need to increase the size of the font used in your novel and/or decide to use a smaller printed page size to increase the number of pages in the finished book.

3. Printing Costs

Larger pages mean that you can get more words printed per page and the total number of pages in the book will be smaller, cutting down printing costs and increasing your profit on book sales. But you should balance out the risk that the page count for the book will drop so low that you cannot have a spine on your book.

4. Your genre or niche – and hence marketability

Books in specific niches have also developed their own styling and design elements which readers expect to see for a book in that niche.

These include font selection, content layout, image placement and book cover design.

You should make yourself familiar with other books in your niche so that your book will be consistent with niche branding.

If you survey the commercial paperback books for your niche on Amazon, in your local bookstore or airport bookstore, they tend to be the same size with very similar artwork, title fonts and colour schemes.

There are very clear expectations about the size of paperback books in specific genres. For example. Harlequin romances are published in series every month and romance fans expect mass market paperbacks which are consistently 4.2" x 6.5" in size.

If every other book in your niche is being sold at a trim size, for example, of 5.25" x 8" for a similar number of pages to your manuscript, then you need to have a good reason why you want to produce a different size paperback.

Think about your bookcase at home. How do you arrange your personal collection of books? Usually it is with the spine facing out and by the height of the book.

Think about how your book will fit onto a reader's bookshelf with the top 20 or 50 novels in your genre.

Common Trim Sizes for Commercial Paperback Print Books

Commercial books are printed in the US by traditional publishers as "**trade paperbacks**." Trade paperback sizes will range anywhere from 5.5" x 8.5", also known as Digest, to 6" x 9", also known as US Trade.

In today's market, 6" x 9" is the most popular paperback size for many novels, memoirs, and non-fiction books.

Short novels, novellas and commercial fiction such as romance and crime novels are normally smaller in size such as 5" by 8" or 5.25"x 8".

In the UK, mass market paperbacks are often produced in what are known as A, B or C format sizes:

A format paperback is 11.1 x 17.8cm. (4.33" x 7.01")

B format paperbacks are 12.9 x 19.8cm. (5.25" x 7.75")

C format (Demy) paperbacks are typically 135mm x 216mm (5.32" x 8.51")

A4 books are 21.0 x 29.7 cm. (8.27" x 11.69")

A5 books are 14.8 x 21.0 cm. (5.83" x 8.27")

Children's books and Illustrated books such as cookbooks tend to be larger at 8" x 10", 8.5" x 11" or square 8.5" x 8.5". Often they have custom dimensions to accommodate the extra wide artwork and photographs.

5. The ideal reading experience you want for your reader.

In general, the larger the word count in your book, the bigger you can go with the trim size, since this will reduce the page count and make it easier for the reader to hold the book and be able to read the text at a legible font size without eye strain.

For example, *Harry Potter and the Sorcerer's Stone* comes in around 336 pages and was published by Arthur A. Levine Books as a 5.2" x 8" paperback. Ideal for carrying around and easy to pick up and read in one hand.

On the other hand, *Cat in the Hat* is 64 pages long and Random House created a 7.4" x 9.4" paperback for children to enjoy the full-colour illustrations.

HOW TO DECIDE ON THE IDEAL PAGE SIZE FOR YOUR BOOK?

The best tip is to research examples of books in your niche and use the same dimensions for your print paperback book – provided that your manuscript has a similar number of pages at that trim size, of course.

It will only take a few minutes to note down the dimensions of the top 20 to 50 paperbacks for your niche market and the number of print pages.

The dimensions of all print books on Amazon are displayed in the Product Details section on the book description page for that book.

Readers will expect to be offered books of similar size in that particular book category.

NOTE. Your page size is not fixed. You can edit the size of your document at any time and create a new manuscript by changing the page size of your Word document.

For example: for the case study novel.

MURDER AND MOZZARELLA: A Kingsmede Cozy Mystery Paperback

Paperback: 219 pages. **Product Dimensions:** 5.1 x 0.5 x 7.8 inches

What trim sizes do KDP print paperbacks offer?

There are minimum and maximum number of pages specified for each standard and non-standard trim size – but don't forget that the ability to use custom print dimensions is one of the major advantages of using KDP print which is rarely offered by commercial print on demand companies. Be consistent though and stick to the market conventions.

KDP Print Trim Sizes

TRIM SIZE Inches and Centimetres	BLACK INK ON WHITE PAPER Page Count	BLACK INK ON CREAM PAPER Page Count	COLOR INK ON WHITE PAPER Page Count
5" x 8" (12.7 x 20.32 cm)	24-828	24-776	24-828
5.06" x 7.81" (12.85 x 19.84 cm)	24-828	24-776	24-828
5.25" x 8" (13.34 x 20.32 cm)	24-828	24-776	24-828
5.5" x 8.5" (13.97 x 21.59 cm)	24-828	24-776	24-828
6" x 9" (15.24 x 22.86 cm)	24-828	24-776	24-828
6.14" x 9.21" (15.6 x 23.39 cm)	24-828	24-776	24-828
6.69" x 9.61" (16.99 x 24.4 cm)	24-828	24-776	24-828
7" x 10" (17.78 x 25.4 cm)	24-828	24-776	24-828
7.44" x 9.69" (18.9 x 24.61 cm)	24-828	24-776	24-828
7.5" x 9.25" (19.05 x 23.5 cm)	24-828	24-776	24-828
8" x 10" (20.32 x 25.4 cm)	24-828	24-776	24-828
8.25" x 6" (20.96 x 15.24 cm)	24-800	24-750	24-800
8.25" x 8.25" (20.96 x 20.96 cm)	24-800	24-750	24-800
8.5" x 8.5" (21.59 x 21.59 cm)	24-590	24-550	24-590
8.5" x 11" (21.59 x 27.94 cm)	24-590	24-550	24-590
8.27" x 11.69" (21 x 29.7 cm)	24-780	24-730	Not available

As you can see from the chart, KDP Print offers a very wide variety of print sizes.

There is one proviso. If you want Amazon KDP to enable Expanded Distribution for your book, so that it can be shipped to bookstores, online retailers, libraries, and academic institutions, it has to meet the following standard KDP trim size eligibility requirements.

This range is constantly being updated, so for the latest information on this option please consult the KDP online reference page. https://amzn.to/3af2fbc

As you can see from the table below, most of the popular sizes for print on demand paperbacks are included in this option for black ink on white paper, with a more limited range for cream paper and colour printing.

Expanded Distribution Trim Size Options

TRIM SIZE Inches and Centimetres	BLACK INK ON WHITE PAPER	BLACK INK ON CREAM PAPER	COLOR INK ON WHITE PAPER
5" x 8" (12.7 x 20.32 cm)	Yes	Yes	/
5.06" x 7.81" (12.85 x 19.84 cm)	Yes	/	/
5.25" x 8" (13.34 x 20.32 cm)	Yes	Yes	/
5.5" x 8.5" (13.97 x 21.59 cm)	Yes	Yes	Yes
6" x 9" (15.24 x 22.86 cm	Yes	Yes	Yes
6.14" x 9.21" (15.6 x 23.39 cm)	Yes	/	Yes
6.69" x 9.61" (16.99 x 24.4 cm)	Yes	/	/
7" x 10" (17.78 x 25.4 cm)	Yes	/	Yes
7.44" x 9.69" (18.9 x 24.61 cm)	Yes	/	/
7.5" x 9.25" (19.05 x 23.5 cm)	Yes	/	/
8" x 10" (20.32 x 25.4 cm)	Yes	/	Yes
8.5" x 8.5" (21.59 x 21.59 cm)	/	/	Yes
8.5" x 11" (21.59 x 27.94 cm)	Yes	/	Yes

HOW TO SET THE PAGE SIZE FOR YOUR BOOK

Unless you are using the default page sizes of A4 or US Letter as the trim size for your finished paperback, once you have decided on the ideal size for your book, it's time to change the page size of your manuscript to match the trim size.

Don't wait until the end of the formatting process to change the paper dimensions for your document. Doing it now will make it much easier to format your print format book.

Follow the instructions for page layout set-up in your text management software.

Microsoft Word

1. Go to the **Layout Tab** in the header.

2. Then click on **Size** and **More Paper Sizes** at the bottom of the options.

3. This will open a pop-up window where you can type in the custom size for your document in the width and height boxes in the default units you have set-up.

4. Click **Apply to the Whole Document**. Then **click OK.**

For example. For a 6" x 9" (15.24 x 22.86 cm) book this would be:

Pages for MacIntosh

1. **Open your Pages document on your Macintosh**.

2. **Click on Document** in the top right header.

3. **Click on the up/down chevron tab** next to US Letter (or A4) **in the Printer and Paper Size bar.** This will show you the default size you have set up.

4. Then go to **File in the Upper Left Header and click on Page Setup** in the drop-down menu.

5. **Click on the Manage Custom Sizes option** in the pop-up window.

6. **Click the + button to add a new size.**

7. **Type in the dimensions for your new paper size in the Width and Height boxes.**

8. **Then type in a shortcut name in the text box** for this style on the left. **Then click OK.**

To see the change in your document, click on **View** in the header bar and then **Show Ruler and Show Layout.**

If you wish you can also go to **File** in the Upper Left Header and click on **Save as Template** in the drop-down menu.

Then **Add to Template** Chooser in the pop-up box. Give your new page template a name in the Template Options.

In Google Docs.

1. Open up your Google docs. document.

2. **Click on File** in the header bar then click on **Page Setup**.

3. Then click on **Paper Size** in the pop-up box.

4. You will have a drop-down menu of a limited range of 11 paper sizes.

5. Select the option you want. Then OK.

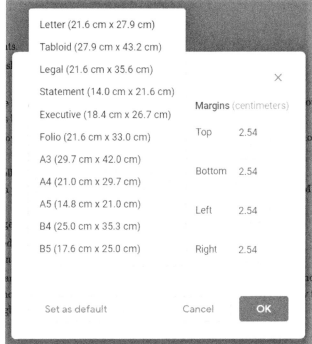

As you can see, at the time of writing this guide, the range of page sizes for Google docs. is limited and fits only 3 of the KDP standard trim sizes.

AMAZON KDP STANDARD TRIM SIZE

5.5" x 8.5" (13.97 x 21.59 cm)

8.5" x 11" (21.59 x 27.94 cm)

8.27" x 11.69" (21 x 29.7 cm)

If you don't want to use those dimensions, then at this point it may be better to export your Google Docs. file into a Word document so that you can use the additional paper dimensions options and styling available.

CHECK THE PAGE COUNT FOR YOUR BOOK

Once you have reset the page size of your document, check the number of pages this change to your document has created.

If you don't have at least 100 to 120 double-sided printed pages, you will need to consider a smaller page size or using a larger body text font to ensure that the finished paperback will be thick enough to have lettering on the spine.

9

DECIDE ON THE MARGINS FOR YOUR PRINT BOOK

SETTING THE MARGINS FOR YOUR BOOK

Once you have the ideal trim size for your book and know approximately how many pages your book will be, you need to start laying out your pages for print.

Every page in a printed book has 5 margins which sets the distance between the text of your novel and the edge of the page.

• A top margin. This is where the header text will be contained.

• A bottom margin. This is where any footer text will be contained.

• An outside margin.

• An inside margin.

• An extra inside "gutter" margin.

The gutter is the gap in the fold of the printed book between the right and left pages where the pages will be glued or stitched together.

This additional gutter space is to make sure that the text of your novel does not get lost into this gap during the binding process, making it impossible to read.

The total inside margin of every page will therefore be the combination of both the inside margin width and the gutter margin width that you set.

This is why print books have "**mirror margins**" where the gutter is equal on both right and left pages which are reflections of one another.

Top tip. If you want to see where the margins are in your Word document, go to the **Home tab,** then **click View** then click **Show Gridlines**.

This will show you where your text lies in the book and where the margins are for that text. Visualising that space can be a big help in setting realistic margins.

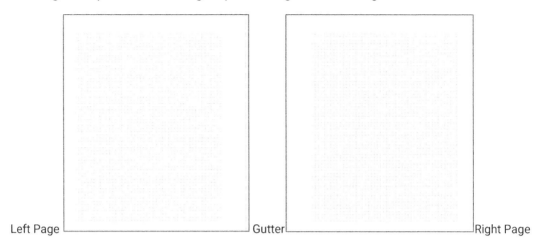

Left Page   Gutter   Right Page

Amazon KDP does have some recommended minimum settings for book margins which you can use as a guide.

Note: The term "bleed" refers to book elements such as images which extend outside the margins to the very edge of the page. This does not apply to most novels where the body text will fit between the margins of your page.

Hence these guidelines are for text without bleed (no bleed).

Amazon KDP Minimum Margin sizes

Page Count	Inside (Gutter) Margins	Outside Margins (no bleed)
24 to 150 pages	0.375" (9.6 mm)	at least 0.25" (6.4 mm)
151 to 300 pages	0.5" (12.7 mm)	at least 0.25" (6.4 mm)
301 to 500 pages	0.625" (15.9 mm)	at least 0.25" (6.4 mm)
501 to 700 pages	0.75" (19.1 mm)	at least 0.25" (6.4 mm)
701 to 828 pages	0.875" (22.3 mm)	at least 0.25" (6.4 mm)

Microsoft Word

1. Go to the **Layout Tab** in the Page Setup header menu

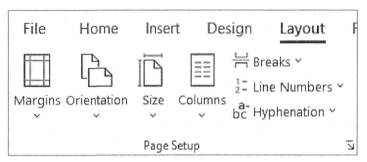

2. Then click on **Margins** and then **Custom Margins** at the bottom of the options.

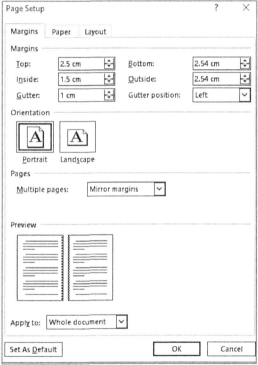Example Page Setup.

3. This will open a pop-up window where you can type in the custom size for your document in the width and height boxes in the default units you have set-up. The software will automatically recognise that these are custom dimensions.

4. Click **Pages**. **Multiple pages** and then select **Mirror Margins**.

This will ensure that the gutter space is applied equally on both the right and left pages of your book.

5. Click **Apply to the Whole Document**. Then **click OK.**

In Google Docs.

1. Open up your Google docs. document.

2. **Click on File** in the header bar under the **Editing** Option then click on **Page Setup**.

3. You will have a drop-down menu of all four margin settings.

4. Type in the margin size you want. Then **OK**.

You can change these margins at any time to accommodate changes in the space needed in the headers and footers of your document.

For example, smaller trim size books do not need large top, bottom or outside margins and these can be adjusted to create a perfect frame for the text.

In addition, most authors have their name and the title of the book on alternate pages in the headers in the book and the page number in the footer of the page.

Other authors prefer to add the page number to the header of each page. This means that you do not need such a large footer and you could decrease the size of the bottom margin accordingly, creating more space for the text of your novel.

We will cover this in more detail when we format the headers and footers of your book.

10

DECIDE ON THE NORMAL BODY TEXT STYLE FOR YOUR PRINT BOOK

One important aspect of creating a consistent reading experience for your customer is to use the same book styles throughout your book.

If you look at Amazon reviews for indie-published books, many readers complain about abrupt changes in formatting or breaks in the text. Sudden changes in the text is going to distract your reader and pull them out of the reading experience, just when they are enjoying your content!

Deciding on the standard styles for your text at this stage in the formatting will also save you a lot of time as you work through your book.

There are two key styles which should be set before formatting any print book:

#Your Normal Style for the body text of your novel.

#The Chapter Heading Style.

Set the Normal Body Style

If you have removed all the formatting, the text of your book will already be set to the "Normal" style. Now is the time to update the Normal style to reflect the interior design you have created for this book.

Step One. Font and Font Size

Each font will look different, even with the same font size, so I would recommend experimenting with a few different standard serif fonts until you have the combination of font and font size that works best for your particular book project.

Reminder. Serif fonts have small tails at the end of the letters. Non-serif fonts are cleaner and straighter in style.

For example. For most novels, readers will have a better reading experience of large amounts of text when you use a serif style font in font size 10, 11 or 12 point.

I would recommend changing the Normal style of your novel to a classic serif font from the start which makes it easy for your readers to enjoy the novel.

Standard serif styles include **Garamond 12**, Palatino 12, Georgia 12 and Times New Roman 12 point, but there are many others.

How to change the Normal Style of your document.

Select a few paragraphs of text from a chapter in your book. The style of that text will display in the Styles header bar.

In Word.

Change the font and font size of your text until you are happy with it.

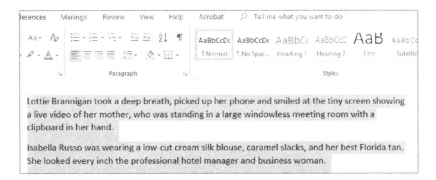

In this example I want to change the font from Calibri 11point to Georgia 11point.

Click on the **Normal** style which should be highlighted then click on **Update Normal to Match Selection.**

Your Normal style for the entire document has now been changed.

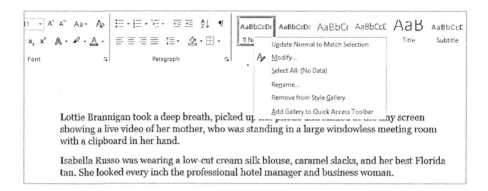

Lottie Brannigan took a deep breath, picked up her phone and smiled at the tiny screen showing a live video of her mother, who was standing in a large windowless meeting room with a clipboard in her hand.

Isabella Russo was wearing a low-cut cream silk blouse, caramel slacks, and her best Florida tan. She looked every inch the professional hotel manager and business woman.

In Google Docs.

Select the text. Check that the header tells you that this is the Normal text style.

In this example the current font is Arial 11 point. Let's change it to Georgia 11 point.

Click **Update 'Normal text' to match**.

Step Two. The Paragraph First Line Indent

This does not usually apply to non-fiction books where paragraphs are usually left aligned with a line space between paragraphs. Many novelists, however, prefer to indent the text on the first line of each paragraph using a hanging indent paragraph style.

Using the same example of chapter text, let's set a hanging indent for the first line of each paragraph of 0.3cm.

In Word.

1. Select a few paragraphs of body text from your novel.

2. Click on the **Home tab**, then **Paragraph** options in your header bar.

3. Then set the **Special First Line indentation** to 0.3cm (or the equivalent in the US) and **click OK** to insert the paragraph indent.

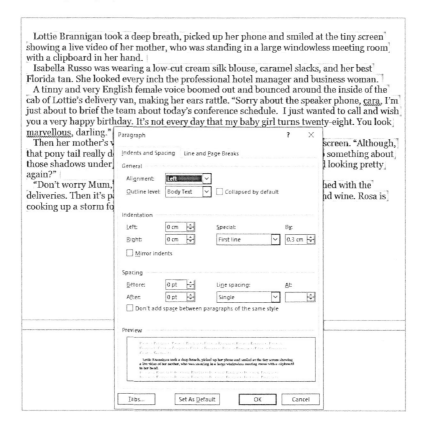

Many fiction authors prefer to use a different first line indent of 0.2 or 0.4 cm so feel free to experiment with a large block of text to see how changing the first line indent impacts both the appearance and the reading experience of your book.

Remember – you need to be consistent across the entire manuscript, so decisions at this point will impact the remainder of your book.

See how your chapter looks and if you want a larger indent, simply repeat the process and increase the indent in the first line in the paragraph formatting styles.

In Google Docs.

1. Select a few paragraphs of text. Go to the **Format** option in the header bar, then **Align and Indent.**

2. Select the **Indentation Options** and then **Special, First Line** and set the indent size.

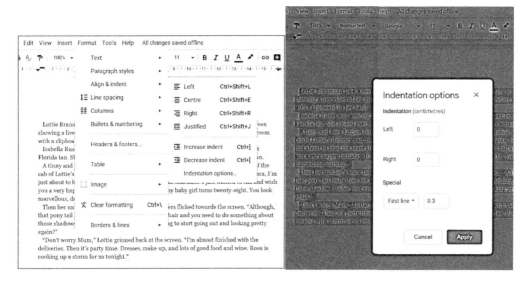

Step Three. Text Alignment

This is very much personal choice.

Some authors prefer to leave the body text left aligned, while others prefer to fully justify the text of their novel so that it automatically fills the page with blocks of text. This can cause problems where you only have a few words on a page.

Example of left aligned indented text.

***

Lottie Brannigan took a deep breath, picked up her phone and smiled at the tiny screen showing a live video of her mother, who was standing in a large windowless meeting room with a clipboard in her hand.

Isabella Russo was wearing a low-cut cream silk blouse, caramel slacks, and her best Florida tan. She looked every inch the professional hotel manager and businesswoman.

***

Example of the same indented text which has been fully justified.

***

Lottie Brannigan took a deep breath, picked up her phone and smiled at the tiny screen showing a live video of her mother, who was standing in a large windowless meeting room with a clipboard in her hand.

Isabella Russo was wearing a low-cut cream silk blouse, caramel slacks, and her best Florida tan. She looked every inch the professional hotel manager and businesswoman.

***

To change the alignment of your normal body text from left aligned to justified, use the same instructions as in the previous change.

In Word.

1. Select a few paragraphs of body text from your manuscript.

2. Click on the **Home tab**, then **Paragraph options** in your header bar.

3. Then select the **Alignment** option and change to **Justified.**

This will change the body style wherever you use the Normal text setting.

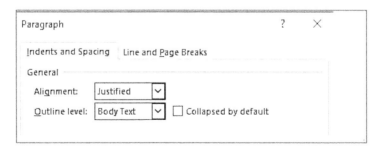

In Google Docs.

1. Select a few paragraphs of text.

2. Go to the **Format** option in the header bar, then **Align and Indent**.

3. Select the **Justified** option.

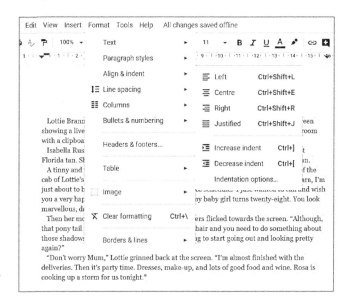

Apply the Normal style to the body text of your book

1. Place the cursor before the chapter one title header and then hold down the SHIFT + PAGE DOWN keys until the cursor moves to the end of your document.

2. Keep everything highlighted. On the **Home** tab, in the **Styles** ribbon, click the **Normal** style.

Tip: Applying the Normal style to all the content from chapter one onwards, ensures that any remaining hidden or unintentional formatting in the body text of your book is automatically changed to the same normal style you have just created.

11

CREATING THE CHAPTER HEADING STYLE

DECIDE ON THE CHAPTER HEADING STYLE FOR YOUR BOOK

It is essential that all chapter titles and section headings should be marked as Header 1 style if you want them to be included in the Table of Contents.

For example.   **In Word.** The chapter one heading is currently in Normal.

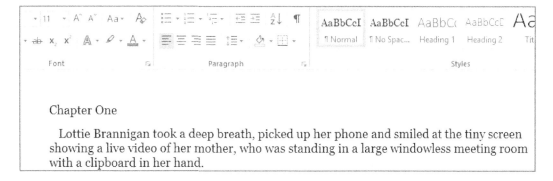

In both Word and Google Docs. simply click at the chapter or page heading and select Heading 1 style in the Styles menu or list.

You can set the font and font size of any chapter heading to match your genre and the overall style that you are looking for in your book.

Step One. Decide on Chapter Headings Font and Font Size.
Now you can have fun and experiment with fonts and font sizes until you find the perfect match for your book.

You can use any fonts you like, provided that you have the licence to use that font commercially and Amazon KDP will print it in your PDF.

Here are a few options, for example, for the chapter headings of my cozy mystery novel.

Lucida Handwriting 18 point. *Chapter One*

Or Century Schoolbook 20 point. Chapter One

Or Georgia 18 point. Chapter One

Or Gloucester MT Extra Condensed 24 point. **Chapter One**

The idea is to create something which is good fit for your genre and your book.

<u>**To Set the Heading 1 Style in Word**</u>

1. Select the chapter heading you have just changed to the font you want to use.

2. Go to the **Styles menu** in the **Home tab** and right click on the **Heading 1 style.**

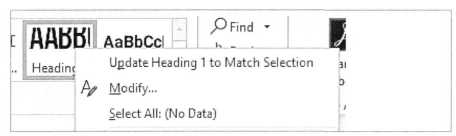

3. Click on **Update Heading 1 to Match Selection**.

The font and paragraph formatting for Heading 1 will now be in place for the document.

<u>**In Google Docs.**</u>

1. Select the chapter heading.

2. Click on the **Normal text** header and click the down arrow to **select Heading 1,** then **Apply 'Heading 1'.**

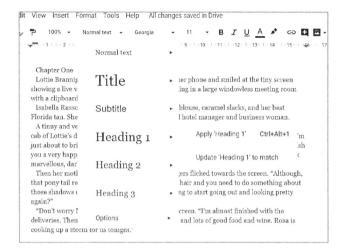

If you change your mind and decide on another font you can change all of the headings automatically by changing the Heading 1 style.

To Update Heading 1. Select the chapter heading that you have just customised with the font that you want to use. Then click **Update Heading 1 to match.**

Step Two. Set the Heading 1 Spacing and Alignment

The heading of every new chapter or section page in a printed book is normally dropped about a third of the way down the page and placed in the centre of the page.

Space is also inserted below the chapter heading to separate it from the first paragraph of text. How much space you insert before and after your headings will depend on the trim size of your book and the font size you have chosen.

The best thing to do is experiment and see what the results look like.

In Word.

1. **On the Home tab, right-click the Heading 1 style and select Modify. This opens a dialog box.**

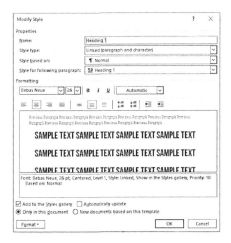

2. Click the **Format** option at the bottom left and select **Paragraph.**

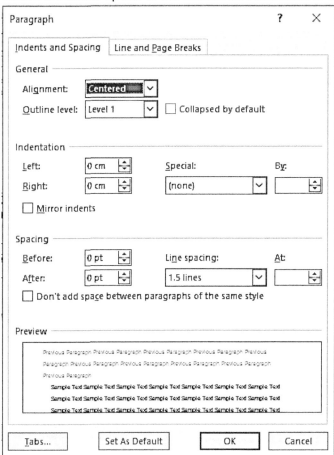

3.   Under **Special, select (none).**

4.   Under **Spacing, set Before and After to 60pt.**

5.   The **Line Spacing** refers to the **line spacing of the text** of your chapter title and is usually set between single or 1.5 lines.

6.   **Alignment.** Most chapter headings are **aligned centrally** on the page, but you can change this if you prefer left aligned chapter headings for your particular novel.

Click OK on both open boxes to save changes.

Review what the chapter heading looks like on the page and either accept this spacing or go back and modify the Heading 1 paragraph style again until the spacing is how you want it.

In Google Docs.

1.   **Highlight the Chapter heading.**

2.   **On the Format tab, click Line Spacing and select Custom Spacing.** This opens a dialog box where you can type in the spacing before and after your chapter heading.

3.   Then click **Apply.**

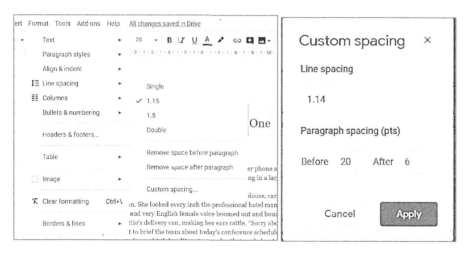

Now work through the document and apply the saved Heading 1 style to every chapter title and page title that you want to be included in the table of contents for your novel.

Don't forget to save your updated document.

12

FORMATTING THE FRONT MATTER OF YOUR BOOK

COMPONENTS OF A PRINT BOOK

THE FRONT MATTER.

This is also called the **Preliminary Matter**. Basically, the front matter is everything that precedes the main text of your novel.

The Front Matter can include:

• **The Copyright page.**

• **Praise for the book** from leading authors in your niche. (Optional) These reviews can also be listed as editorial reviews on the Amazon book description page.

• **Dedication.** (Optional)This is the personal dedication written by the author.

• **About the book.** (Optional)This is written by the author and should set out the scope and objectives of the book, especially if this novel is part of a series.

• **Note from the Author**. Optional but very useful for indie authors. This is where you can offer a "reader magnet" freebie when the reader subscribes to your mailing list. The intention is to invite readers from Amazon to click over to your website or a landing page/ opt-in page which you control. If you have this invitation early in the book, it will be included in the "Look Inside" sample. Note. This is also repeated in the back matter at the end of the book so that you can capture the email address of your readers.

• **Acknowledgements.** (Optional) Many indie authors move this to the back of the book so that the sample "look inside" pages of the book include the opening pages of the text.

• **Table of Contents/Contents.** The wording of each entry should match the headings in the text of the book.

• **Lists of illustrations, figures and maps.** (Optional) Especially useful for children's books and fantasy novels.

• **Epigraph Quotation.** (Optional)An epigraph is a relevant quotation which is added to the start of the book, or each chapter or part of the book. It is formatted differently from the rest of the text so that it stands out.

THE BODY TEXT. These are the chapters and main text of your book.

THE BACK MATTER. This is also called the **End Matter**. This is everything that comes after the main text of your book, and can include any references, appendices, a list of other books by the author and an "About the Author" page.

Creating the Book Interior

In this chapter are going to start going through the manuscript and transform each section of the book into a print book.

First - Some Terminology and Formatting Rules for Print books.

Rule1. Each Part of the Front Matter Begins on a new Right-Hand Page

Recto = the right-hand side page of the book when it is opened up, which is always given an odd page number.

Verso = a left-hand page when the book is opened up, which is always given an even page number.

The main text of the book and any major new part usually starts on a right hand, recto page, even if it means leaving a blank left-hand page.

The reason for this rule is simply because the reader will automatically start reading on the right-hand page of a book, so all of the important information should be on a right-hand page which is always given an odd page number.

Rule 2. Each New Part of the Front Matter traditionally does not have a page number, header or footer on the first page.

This means, for example, that if you have included an Author Note or Table of Contents which is two or more pages long, then the first page will not have a page number, header of footer but the second and subsequent pages will.

Rule 3. The page numbers for the Front Matter are separate from the rest of the book.

The front matter pages are usually numbered with lower case Roman numerals (i, ii, iii…etc.) so that they are different from the main text, which is numbered using Arabic numerals (1,2,3…etc.). It also means that you can edit the front matter pages without impacting the page numbering in the rest of the book.

Many indie authors ignore this rule, but it does add a professional touch to non-fiction printed books and longer fiction books.

Front Matter Examples

Worked Examples from Case Study. A Short Mystery Novel

The Copyright Page is on the reverse of the Title Page of the printed book.

About this Book.

This is the first book in a new cozy mystery series, and I wanted the readers to recognise that the second book was already written and available.

Readers love series and prefer to invest their time in a book where others in the series are available to purchase immediately.

There is an exclusive sample of the beginning of book two at the end of this book and a link to the Amazon page for the book.

Invitation to join a Reader Mailing List.

I offer free books and bonuses to my mailing list subscribers through the Sophie Brent website.

MURDER AND MOZZARELLA

SOPHIE BRENT

COZY MYSTERY AUTHOR

ABOUT THIS BOOK

The 1st book in the NEW Kingsmede Cozy Murder Mystery series!

What do you do when your elderly Italian godmother is accused of murdering the chef brought in to replace her – and she probably did it?

This book will delight fans of TV shows like 'Midsomer Murders' and 'Murder She Wrote' who love reading cozy mysteries such as the Agatha Raisin and Peridale Café series.

Lottie Brannigan thought that life was complicated enough when all she had to cope with were her friends and the latest antics of her Italian relatives, but then she finds her neighbor knocked out on his doorstep and her godmother is accused of murdering a rival chef!
Running an Italian deli in an English country village has never been so deadly!
***

WOULD YOU LIKE *FREE* COPIES OF FUTURE BOOKS BY SOPHIE BRENT, EXCLUSIVE NEWS AND GIVEAWAYS?
Pop along to my website and join my Reader Group!
SophieBrent.com

13

FORMATTING THE TITLE PAGE OF YOUR BOOK

The Title Page.

This has the title of your book, a subtitle, if you are using one, and your name as the author. You can also add an author or publisher brand image on the title page.

Font Selection

Traditional publishers often use the same fonts or original artwork that were used on the book cover for the main title page of the book. This is an elegant detail and adds to the quality professional style of your book.

Here is an example of a romance cover mock-up image for a front cover design and the matching title page. There are only two fonts used in the cover design (Playfair Display in italics and Glacial Indifference) but against the background image they can be very effective.

Font Size

The general guideline is to use a large font size for the main title, a smaller size for any subtitle and then a different font for the author name.

This does vary according to genre. Some authors have developed a powerful author brand and their name may be prominently displayed on both the book cover and the title page.

If you have decided to buy your own ISNB number and created your own publisher name, then this can be added in a smaller font at the bottom of the title page together with any publisher logo or image you want to use.

Formatting the Title Page of your Novel

Use the Font and Paragraph Tabs in the header bar to customise the styling of your title page. Each element is formatted separately.

Worked Example. This is the title page from the manuscript of Murder and Mozzarella.

In Word.

1. **Highlight the title text of your book.**

2. **Click the Font option in the Home tab**. A pop-up window will appear.

3. **Change the font** to the one that best fits your book cover fonts and increase the size to at least 24 point. Change to all caps, small caps or italics as you prefer. The size of the font will also depend on the trim size of your book. Super large titles will swamp a smaller book. So, consider the spacing on the page.

4. Then **OK.**

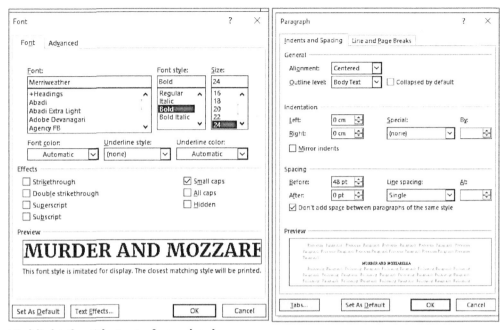

5. **Highlight the title text of your book.**

6. **Click the Paragraph option in the Home tab.** A pop-up window will appear.

7. **Alignment.** Should be Centred.

8. **Spacing.** You want the main title to be about a third of the way down the page.

   In this case I used a 48point space before the title text.
   The actual line spacing I kept as Single because the title was on two lines.

Formatting the subtitle text of your book and/or your author name.

Repeat the two steps above for any subtitle text and your author name.

For example. To format the Author Name.

1. **Highlight the author name text.**

2. **Click the Font option in the Home tab**. A pop-up window will appear.

Change the font to the one that best fits your book cover fonts and set the size to at least 14 point. Change to all caps, small caps or italics as you prefer. Then OK.

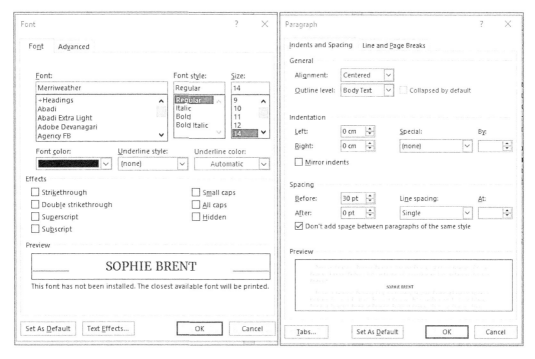

3. **Click the Paragraph option in the Home tab.** A pop-up window will appear.

4. **Alignment.** Should be Centred.

5. **Spacing.** You want the author name to be about at least halfway down the page or lower.

In this case I used a 30point space between the bottom of the title text and where the author name begins. The actual line spacing I kept as Single.

Check to see how your book title appears on the page and repeat these two steps until you are happy with it.

It may take several attempts before you find the perfect spacing and font that perfectly matches your genre which you know will appeal to your ideal reader.

Top Tip. Model your inspiration on bestselling titles in your niche. Use the "Look Inside" feature on the Amazon book page for these titles and review how they lay out the title page in their print books and evaluate if that styling is a good fit for your book.

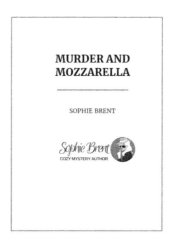

In Google Docs.

Repeat the same steps I have just described for Word, using Styles and Format options to change the font and alignment for your book title, subtitle if you are using one and your author name.

1. **Highlight** the title of your book.

2. Click on the **Styles tab** in **Editing** Mode then **Title** and **Apply Title**.

3. Change the font, font size and alignment of your book title.

4. If you want more typefaces than Arial, Georgia, and the other built-in fonts, just click the down arrow on the fonts menu and select *More Fonts*. You can search through all the typefaces in Google Fonts and add them to your Google Docs. account.

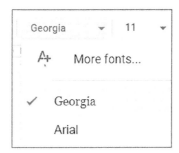

5. Then go to the **Format Tab i**n the header, then **Line Spacing and Custom Spacing** options we went through with chapter headings to set the distance above and below each the title text on your title page.

6. Then click on **Update Title to Match** to set the style.

7. Repeat this step for your **Subtitle**.

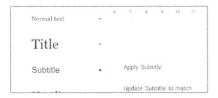

8. For your **Author Name** you can customise the Normal style just for that line or use the Subtitle format if the font and spacing styles work well together.

Images

If you want to add an image to the base of the page.

1. Click on the **Home tab**.

2. Use the **Insert tab** in the header menu and then **Pictures** in the Illustrations menu.

3. **Adjust the size of the image** so that it does not overwhelm the title, subtitle and author name.

Don't forget that your book will be printed in black ink on white or cream paper, so it is a good idea to test what a colour image looks like by printing out the page in black and white. You may find that you have to enlarge the image to make features stand out.

Because you are formatting your work you can select any combination of fonts and styles so that your title page is unique.

14

FORMATTING THE COPYRIGHT PAGE OF YOUR BOOK

The Copyright Page.

On the reverse of the title page is **a short copyright page.**

You will find full details on the Copyright page and ISBN numbers in chapter three of this book.

Copyright Title. The copyright page is not usually included in the Table of Contents, so you don't need to use the Heading 1 style.   You can leave the header style as normal text but in capitals. Or if you want the heading to look the same as the following pages, manually change the font and font size to match Heading 1 but leaving the style as normal.

By convention, the text of the copyright page is centred.

<u>**Formatting the Copyright Page**</u>

In Word.

To make the copyright symbol, hold down the **CTRL + ALT + C** keys. Or use the **Insert tab** and then **Symbols.**

In Google Docs.

Go to the Insert Tab and then Special Characters.

If you cannot find it, use the Search Function to make it easier.

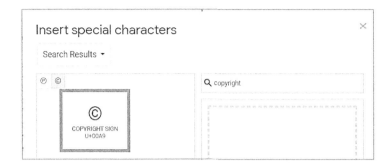

This is where you can also add your own ISBN if you have purchased one and assigned it to this book.

If you choose a free KDP Print Paperback ISBN, the number will be added to the back cover and barcode when you start building your book inside KDP.

15

FORMATTING THE DEDICATION AND OTHER FRONT MATTER PAGES OF YOUR BOOK

Formatting the Dedication Page

The dedication is included in the Table of Contents for your book, so you should format the title as Heading 1. The dedication text should be centred on the page.

1. **Highlight the Heading** on the Dedication page.

2. **Click the Styles menu in the Home tab.** Then Click on **Heading 1**.

3. **Select all of the dedication text. Click the Paragraph menu in the Home tab.** Then Click on **Centre.**

Formatting the Other Front Matter Pages

These pages are usually included in the Table of Contents for your novel, so you should format the title of each page as Heading 1.

The text of additional front matter pages retains the normal style.

1. **Highlight the Heading** on the page.

2. **Click the Styles menu in the Home tab.** Then Click on **Heading 1**.

The exception is the Contents page, which is not listed in the Table of Contents, so you don't need to use the Heading 1 style.   You can leave the header style as normal text but in capitals. Or if you want the heading to look the same as the following pages, manually change the font and font size to match Heading 1 but leaving the style as normal.

Page Order in the Front Matter of Printed Books

In chapter six we talked about the formatting rules for print books.

Rule 1. Each Part of the Front Matter Begins on a new Right-Hand Page.

The title page always starts on a right-hand, odd numbered page, such as page 1 or 3.

The copyright page is on the reverse of the title page on an even numbered page.

Each following page in the front matter can be followed by a forced blank page so that the next part of the front matter falls on a right-hand, odd numbered page, such as page 3,5,7 etc.

This means that **The Dedication page is usually followed by a blank page, unless it goes over into two pages in length.**

All of the other Front Matter pages, including The Table of Contents page are followed by a blank page, unless it goes over into two pages.

Using Section Breaks/Next Page - NOT Page Breaks - to create a blank page.

To make sure that the next part of the front matter is on a right-hand page, you insert a section break at the end of the last sentence on the previous page to where you want the blank page to start.

For example. Just after the last word of the text of the dedication.

Each section will then have its own formatting which you can customise to create special page numbers and change the headers and footers.

<u>In Summary.</u>

You insert a Section Break/ Next Page to create a blank page.

To add a Section Break in Word.

1. Place your cursor at the end of the last page of text.

2. Go to the **Layout** tab in the header menu. Then **Breaks**.

3. Then use the down arrow to select **Section Breaks/Next Page.**

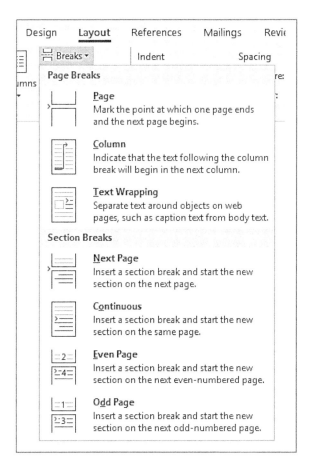

The **Section Break/Next Page** command will insert a blank page and create a new section in the document.

This is important. By convention, the first page of each new part of the front matter does not have a header, footer or page number. By creating a section, you can select the "different first page" setting in the header and footer controls to automatically remove those details from that page. See chapter sixteen for more details.

The typical layout of the opening pages of an indie print book would therefore be as follows:

Page 1	Title page	Must have
Page 2	Copyright page (on the reverse side of the title page)	Must have
Page 3	About this Book or Advance Praise for the book.	Optional
	Insert Section Break. Next Page	
Page 4	Blank page – no headers or footers.	
	Insert Section Break. Next Page	
Page 5	Note from the Author	Optional
	Insert Section Break. Next Page	
Page 6	Blank page – no headers or footers.	
	Insert Section Break. Next Page	
Page 7	Dedication	Optional
	Insert Section Break. Next Page	
Page 8	Blank page – no headers or footers	
	Insert Section Break. Next Page	
Page 9	Table of Contents – one page	Must have
	Insert Section Break. Next Page	
Page 10	Blank page – no headers or footers	
	Insert Section Break. Next Page	

_____

[If the Table of Contents runs onto a second page, then this blank page is not required.]

The page after the Table of Contents marks the end of the Front Matter.

Page 11 will be the first page of chapter one and the main body text of your novel.

Worked Example. Murder and Mozzarella. This book did not have a dedication page.

Pages 1 and 2. Note – this can be confusing, because the page 1 title page is actually on the right-hand side of the page when it is printed in the book.

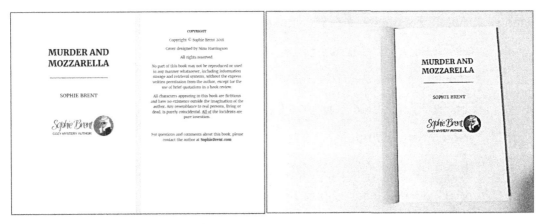

Pages 3 and 4, then Pages 5 and 6.

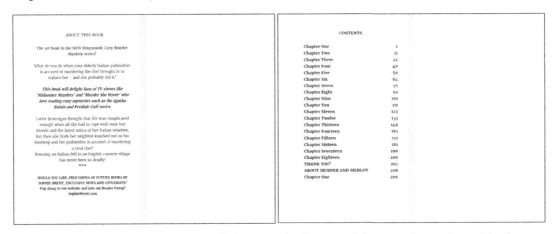

Pages 7 and 8 are the first pages of the main body text of the novel, starting with chapter one.

If you want to check where your section breaks are at any time, go to the **Home tab** and then the **Paragraph** menu. If you click on the **paragraph mark** symbol, this will reveal all of the formatting marks for your document.

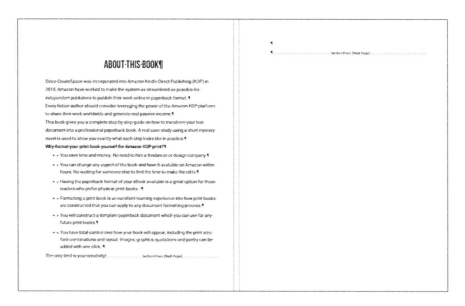

For example. For this book you are reading now. Here are the two **Section Break/Next Page** markers for the About This Book page and then the following blank page in the Front Matter.

Adding Section Breaks in Google Docs.

The exact equivalent of Section Breaks is not an option in Google Docs. to the best of my knowledge.

Different First Page Header/Footer Google Docs.

This only applies the first page of chapter one. All other pages in your document will have the same header and footer/page numbers.

1. Open a document and **Edit Mode.**
2. **Click Insert, Header & page number**.
3. Choose **Header or Footer.**
4. **Enter text into the header or footer**.
5. To make the first page header or footer different from the other pages, check **Different first page header/footer**.

Different headers and footers on alternate pages. This is not an option in Google Docs. to the best of my knowledge.

16

ADDING AND FORMATTING THE PAGE NUMBERS IN THE FRONT MATTER

This will be four stages.

1. **Add the page numbers to your novel.**

2. **Customise the position and font of your page numbers.**

3. **Change the page number format to Roman numbers for the front matter.**

4. **Format the footer to remove the page number from the first page of each section you have created.**

Don't worry! That seems like a lot of detail, but it is actually quite straightforward using the header and footer design tab in Word.

You will recall that there are print-specific rules we need to follow:

Rule 1. Each Part of the Front Matter Begins on a new Right-Hand Page. We covered this in the previous chapter.

Rule 2. Each New Part of the Front Matter traditionally does not have a page number, header or footer on the first page.

Rule 3. The page numbers for the Front Matter are separate from the rest of the book.

We are now going to work through adding and formatting the pages numbers for the front matter step by step, with examples to demonstrate how to do this in Word.

Rule 3. The page numbers for the Front Matter are separate from the rest of the book.

Stage One. Adding Page Numbers

Page numbers are usually used in two positions.

1. At the bottom of the page as part of the footer. This is the most common position for fiction paperbacks.

2. In the upper corners of the top or lower margin as part of the header or footer. (This is the option I used for this book you are reading now.)

For novels, I would recommend keeping it simple and inserting the page numbers at the bottom of the page and in the middle of the page.

In Word

1. **Open your document.**

2. **Click inside the footer of the first page** which usually the title page.

3. This will open a new header and footer **Design tab** in the header bar.

4. Click on the **Insert tab**.

5. Then **Page Number in the Design tab**.

6. Then **Bottom of Page**.

7. You will be then shown a range of positions where you can place the page number.

8. Select the option for the centre of the page. In my version of Word, it is Plain Number 2. **Save** your document.

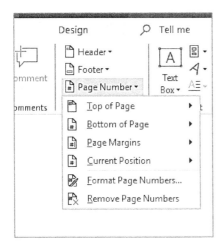

9. You will then see the page number appear at the bottom of the page.

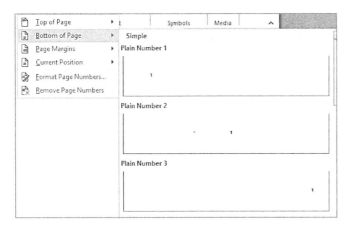

The consecutive page number will not be automatically inserted into the footer of every page in your manuscript.

If you have text in your header or footer, plus the page number, you can align the text with the page number to create the effect that you are looking for.

In Google Docs.

1. **Open your document.**

2. **Click inside the footer of the first page** which usually the title page.

3. **Click the Insert Tab then Header and page number, then Page number.**

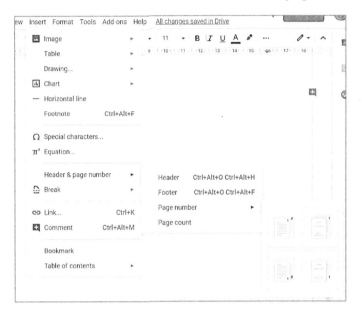

4. You notice the two options on the right – the first page does not have the page number and you can place the page number in the top or bottom corner of the page.

Page number 1 will start on the second page of your document.

5. Then use the **Format tab** then **Align and Indent** to Align the Page number in the location you prefer in the footer or header. Usually the centre of the page.

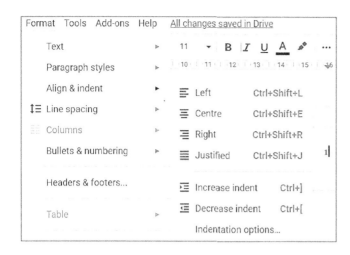

Stage Two. Formatting Page Numbers

Font Size. In most cases the size of the page number will be far too large. Simply click on the number and change the font and the font size until it is small enough to be unobtrusive but large enough to still be seen. **8 or 9 point usually works well**. Save the document to save the new page number size throughout the novel.

Position of the Page Number Footer relative to the Edge of Page

The page number at the bottom of the page is inside the bottom margin of the page which you created earlier.

If the page number is too high relative to the margin and the edge of the page, it will come close to the body text of your novel.

You can set the distance of the footer from the edge of the paper inside the Design Tab in Word.

During the printing process the printed pages will be trimmed, so it is advisable not to have the page number less than 0.5cm from the edge of the paper.

For example, in our case study, the bottom margin was set at 1.78cm.

Compare the appearance of the page number when I decrease the distance from the bottom of the page from 1.27cm to 0.8cm.

This added gap between the bottom of your text and the page number helps the reader to focus on the text of your book and not be distracted by the page number.

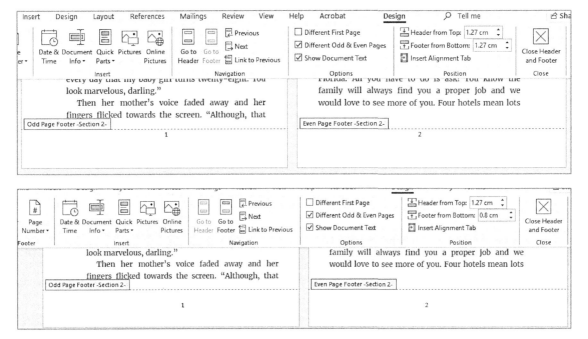

This will, of course, vary according to the trim size you have selected for your print book and the depth of your margins, but it is worth taking the time to experiment with a few different distances from the bottom until you are happy with the appearance of your page number relative to the text.

In Word.

1. **Click on the page number.**

2. This will open up the **Design tab** in the header menu. Then **Position.**

3. Change the distance in the **Footer from Bottom** box.

4. Check that the **Link to Previous** button is live in the **Navigation** menu when the Design tab is open. This will ensure that the page numbers all run consecutively.

In Google Docs.

To set the distance of the page number from the bottom of the paper, click on the page number and use the **Options** setting in the footer or header of your document.

Change the gap and then click **Apply**.

At this point there should be a consecutive page number on every page of your document from the first/title page through to the last page, including the back matter.

Stage Three. Changing the Front Matter Page Numbers to Roman Numbers

If you recall the rule for printed books that we set out in chapter six, the page number system for the front matter of your book is in a different format from the rest of your book.

The default page number style is Arabic numerals: 1,2,3...etc. and this should be used for your entire novel, except for the front matter pages.

The front matter page numbers use the Roman letters in lower case, such as i, ii, iii etc.

Q. How do you separate out the front matter and change the page numbering system?

A. By making each page of the front matter into a different section of the book.

In chapter nine we covered how to insert a blank page after each page in the Front Matter using the **Layout Tab** and **Section Break/Next Page** and not just a simple page break.

The reason for inserting a section break is that every time you create a new section in your document, you can customise the formatting of that section completely separately from any other section in your book, even if it is only two pages.

This allows you to change the style of the page numbers for every section.

In Word. Open your document.

1. **Go the first page/title page of your book and click on the page number.**

2. This will open a new **Design tab** in the header bar which gives you loads of additional information about the page number footer you have created.

   Don't worry about that, just focus on the Header and Footer tab on the left side of the header bar.

3. Click on the **Header and Footer tab**. Then **Page Number.**

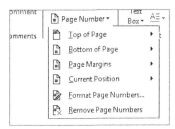

4. Click on **Format Page Numbers... Change the Number format to Roman numerals** by clicking on the little chevron symbol next to the box which says 1,2,3... and selecting i, ii, iii, ...

5. The page number **for this section** should now have been changed to Roman numbers – but the rest of your novel should still be showing 1,2, 3... etc.

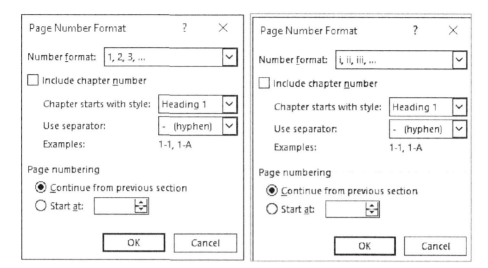

Now you have to repeat this process for every page in the front matter where you have inserted a section break.

The goal is to have every page in the front matter with Roman page numbers, but only the front matter pages. Since this will only be a few pages it is actually very quick to do using the Page Number format tool.

In Google Docs. Sorry, page numbers formats are fixed throughout the document as far as I am aware at this time. This may change in the future.

Almost there!

Now there is one final step in formatting the front matter.

Rule 2. Each New Part of the Front Matter traditionally does not have a page number, header or footer on the first page.

You are not deleting the page numbers, headers and footers, only hiding them from being printed on the first page.

The page numbers will still be counting from the first/title page of your book.

Note – this is only to hide the first page of each section. If any of your front matter contents go over onto two or more pages, then these pages will have the page numbers on the second and later pages of that section.

It is not essential that you do this, but it does look more professional.

Stage Four. Remove the page numbers, headers and footers from the first page of each Front Matter Page

There are two steps.

Step One. You insert another section break on the blank page you have created in chapter nine, just before your text page in the front matter. This will create another section and another blank page.

Delete enough lines on the new blank page to bring up the start of the next front matter page onto that new blank page. How many lines depends on the size of your page etc. You don't want to delete the section break, but you don't need a blank page.

Example from the case study novel for the Contents Page. Note that both pages have lost their page numbers and there are now two section breaks. Before the blank page, section 2 and then one inside the blank page, section 3.

This makes chapter one a new section – section 4.

CONTENTS¶
¶

Chapter·One	→	1¶
Chapter·Two	→	11¶
Chapter·Three	→	22¶
Chapter·Four	→	40¶
Chapter·Five	→	50¶
Chapter·Six	→	64¶
Chapter·Seven	→	75¶
Chapter·Eight	→	92¶
Chapter·Nine	→	101¶
Chapter·Ten	→	111¶
Chapter·Eleven	→	123¶
Chapter·Twelve	→	133¶
Chapter·Thirteen	→	149¶
Chapter·Fourteen	→	161¶
Chapter·Fifteen	→	171¶
Chapter·Sixteen	→	181¶
Chapter·Seventeen	→	190¶
Chapter·Eighteen	→	200¶
THANK·YOU!	→	207¶
ABOUT·MURDER·AND·MERLOT	→	208¶
Chapter·One	→	209¶

..........Section Break (Next Page)..........

..........Section Break (Next Page)..........

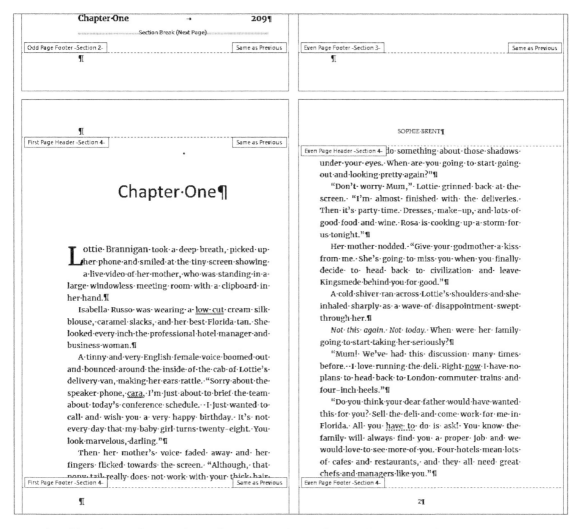

You should only need to do this a few times, depending on how many front matter pages you have in your novel.

By creating these extra sections in the front matter, you have complete control over how you want your headers and footers to appear.

Step Two. You tell Word to make the header and footer Different First Page for the new section that you have created.

In Word. Open your document.

1. **Go the first page/title page of your book and click on the page number at the bottom of the page.**

2. This will open a new **Design tab** in the header bar which gives you loads of additional information about the page number footer you have created.

3. Go to the **Navigation menu.** Make sure that the **Link to Previous** button is live. The page numbers should all be linked and counting in sequence in the Front Matter even if they are hidden and not printed.

4. Go to the **Options menu.**

5. Tick the option marked **Different First Page**. This will blank everything in the headers and footers from the first page **of that section**, including the page number.

6. **Repeat these steps** for all the sections in the front matter.

   Example from the case study novel.

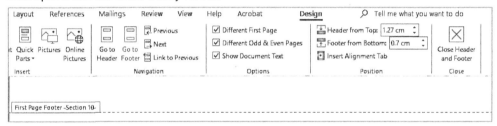

17

FORMATTING THE PAGE NUMBERS FOR THE TEXT

Formatting Page Numbers to Start on Page One of Chapter One

Ideally the page numbers for your novel should start at chapter one or the first page of the actual text of your novel, which could be a quote or a poem of some kind.

In non-fiction books, you can decide to start numbering page on the first page of the introduction to the text, or the first page of the first chapter.

Following on from chapter ten, all of the pages in your novel after the front matter should be in Arabic numerals, 1,2,3, …

In Word

1. **Scroll down to the first page of chapter one of the main text and click on the page number.**

This will open a new **Design tab** in the header bar which gives you loads of additional information about the page number footer you have created. Don't worry about that, just focus on the Header and Footer tab on the left side of the header bar.

2. Click on the **Header and Footer tab**. Then **Page Number.**

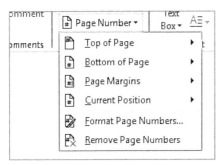

3. Click on **Format Page Numbers...**

4. Change the setting from **Continue from Previous Section** to **Start at...** and use the arrow to select page 1.

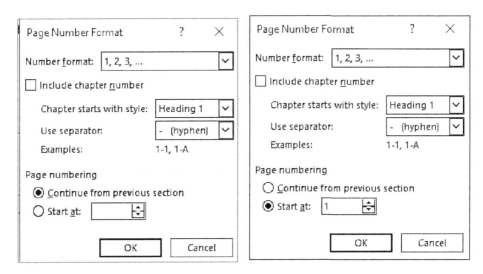

The page numbering for the text of your novel will now start on page one and automatically continue in sequence until the end of the book, including the back matter.

In Google Docs.

The same page number format you set for page one will be in place throughout the document.

18

ADDING AND FORMATTING THE HEADER AND FOOTER TEXT

Traditionally there are two running headers in every novel:

#The name of the author and

#The title of the book.

They are placed in the same line position inside the upper margin space and run continuously on every page, except the front matter and the new chapter pages which may not carry headers.

The name of the author is usually in the header on the left-hand side of the page (the even-number page).

The title of your book is usually in the header on the right-hand side of the page (the odd number page).

It is completely your choice about whether you want to include these two headers in the print format of your novel.

In modern commercial publishing you will find a variety of header styles.

• The positions can be reversed, with the name of the author on the right and the name of the book on the left.

• If the novel is very long and/or each chapter has a name as well as a number, then the name of the book is replaced by the title of each chapter. This is particularly the case for fantasy and children's fiction.

• Some traditional publishers have moved the name of the author and the title of the book to the lower margin so that they become "footers".

• Other publishers have totally removed the header text completely and only use the page numbers in the footer. This is becoming increasingly common with traditional publishers.

It is therefore a personal choice about whether you want to add a header to your book.

I would be guided by the bestsellers in your niche before deciding if headers are needed at all, and if so, the ideal location and style of the header.

Worked example. For our case study mystery novel: the name of the book is **on the right-hand side of the page** (the odd number page) when printed.

MURDER AND MOZZARELLA	SOPHIE BRENT

that, but I can get by with my pals. Please don't worry. I love it here."
    "Then what about your family in London? They miss you. Go and see your uncle Joey. He always has some business idea he could use help with."
	the right decision to take over her father's deli after his death.
	    She needed Brannigan's Deli to work and work brilliantly if she had any hope of building her own business. This was her last chance, her only chance, of creating a life for herself

Adding Headers to Your Book
In Word

1. **Scroll to the first page of chapter one in the main body text part of your book and click inside the upper top margin of the page.**

2. This will open a new **Design tab** in the header bar. And **Options.**

3. Click the box with **Different Odd and Even Pages.** This makes it possible to have different running headers on the right and left facing pages.

4. **Type the Title of your book in the upper margin of the left-hand page of your document**. You can use Upper or Lower Case as you prefer. Some authors like to use the same font that they used in the title of the book, especially if it was a decorative font.

5. **Type your name/the author name in the upper margin of the right-hand page of your document**. Most authors use upper case, but this is personal preference.

Formatting the Header Text

Font and Font Size

The header text should not distract from the text of the novel, so if you do decide to include them, the text should be much smaller than the font size used for the body text.

Position of the Header Text relative to the Edge of Page

In chapter ten we went through how to position the page numbers relative to the edge of the page.

Exactly the same principles apply to the position of the header text.

During the printing process the printed pages will be trimmed, so it is advisable not to have the header text less than 0.5cm from the edge of the paper.

You can set the distance of the header text from the upper edge of the paper inside the **Design Tab in Word.**

Go to the Position menu and type in the gap you want to achieve between the header text and the top edge of the page using the Heading from the Top setting.

For example, in our case study, the top margin was set at 1.78cm. and I selected an upper distance of 0.9cm for this setting.

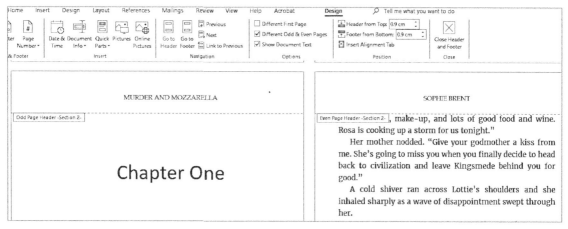

The key objective is to create enough distance between the header and the actual text of your novel, so that the header is not a distraction to the reader.

Creating a Special Format for the First Page of each New Chapter

Many publishers and authors prefer to stay with convention and hide the header and footer on the first page of every new chapter.

To do this, you will need to repeat the process we used in the front matter and make each chapter of your novel into a section of the novel.

You do this by:

• Inserting a "Section break. Next Page" at the end of every chapter, then

• Use the design tab to make the headers and footers of the first page of that section different from the other pages in the chapter.

To hide the page numbers, headers and footers from the first page of every chapter add a Section Break at the end of every chapter.

Follow the same sequence we talked about in chapter ten for the Front Matter.
In Word. Open your document.

1. Go the last line on the last page of chapter one.

2. Place your cursor at the end of the last page of text.

3. Go to the **Layout** tab in the header menu. Then **Breaks**.

4. Then use the down arrow to select **Section Breaks, Next Page.** This will insert a blank page and create a new section in the document.

5. You don't want a blank page between the end of the chapter and the start of the new one. **Delete enough lines on the new blank page to bring up the start of the next chapter onto that new page.** How many lines depends on the size of your page etc. so you will need to experiment. You don't want to delete the section break, but you don't need a blank page.

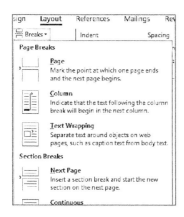

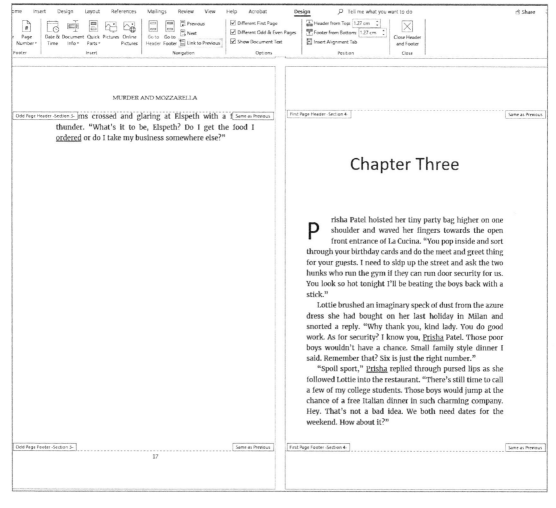

ms crossed and glaring at Elspeth with a thunder. "What's it to be, Elspeth? Do I get the food I ordered or do I take my business somewhere else?"

Chapter Three

P risha Patel hoisted her tiny party bag higher on one shoulder and waved her fingers towards the open front entrance of La Cucina. "You pop inside and sort through your birthday cards and do the meet and greet thing for your guests. I need to skip up the street and ask the two hunks who run the gym if they can run door security for us. You look so hot tonight I'll be beating the boys back with a stick."

Lottie brushed an imaginary speck of dust from the azure dress she had bought on her last holiday in Milan and snorted a reply. "Why thank you, kind lady. You do good work. As for security? I know you, Prisha Patel. Those poor boys wouldn't have a chance. Small family style dinner I said. Remember that? Six is just the right number."

"Spoil sport," Prisha replied through pursed lips as she followed Lottie into the restaurant. "There's still time to call a few of my college students. Those boys would jump at the chance of a free Italian dinner in such charming company. Hey. That's not a bad idea. We both need dates for the weekend. How about it?"

<u>Use the design tab to make the headers and footers of the first page of that section different from the other pages in the chapter.</u>

In Word. Open your document.

1. **Go the first page of chapter one.** Chapter one should already be a new section of the book, because you inserted a section break after the table of contents in the front matter.

2. **Click in the header at the top of the page.**

3. This will open a new **Design tab** in the header bar which gives you loads of additional information about the page number footer you have created.

4. Go to the **Options menu.**

5. Tick the option marked **Different First Page**. This will blank everything in the headers and footers from the first page of that section, including the page number.

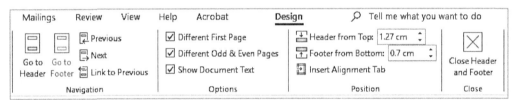

Then repeat this process for the first page of every chapter in your novel which you have just made into a separate section.

Don't worry – it only takes a few minutes per chapter and it does get quicker the more you practice on your document.

At the end of this step, you should have hidden the headers and footers from the first page of every new chapter in the book. This will create a more professional appearance for your work and demonstrate your understanding of publishing standard practices.

Example from the case study novel with the **Design tab** live.

First Page Header -Section 2-   Same as Previous

Chapter One

Lottie Brannigan took a deep breath, picked up her phone and smiled at the tiny screen showing a live video of her mother, who was standing in a large windowless meeting room with a clipboard in her hand.

Isabella Russo was wearing a low-cut cream silk blouse, caramel slacks, and her best Florida tan. She looked every inch the professional hotel manager and business woman.

A tinny and very English female voice boomed out and bounced around the inside of the cab of Lottie's delivery van, making her ears rattle. "Sorry about the speaker phone, cara, I'm just about to brief the team about today's conference schedule. I just wanted to call and wish you a very happy birthday. It's not every day that my baby girl turns twenty-eight. You look marvelous, darling."

Then her mother's voice faded away and her fingers flicked towards the screen. "Although, that pony tail really does not work with your thick hair and you need to do something about those shadows under your eyes. When are you going to start going out and looking pretty again?"

"Don't worry Mum," Lottie grinned back at the screen. "I'm almost finished with the deliveries. Then it's party

First Page Footer -Section 2-   Same as Previous

Even Page Header -Section 2- , make-up, and lots of good food and wine. Rosa is cooking up a storm for us tonight."

Her mother nodded. "Give your godmother a kiss from me. She's going to miss you when you finally decide to head back to civilization and leave Kingsmede behind you for good."

A cold shiver ran across Lottie's shoulders and she inhaled sharply as a wave of disappointment swept through her.

Not this again. Not today. When were her family going to start taking her seriously?

"Mum! We've had this discussion many times before. I love running the deli. Right now I have no plans to head back to London commuter trains and four-inch heels."

"Do you think your dear father would have wanted this for you? Sell the deli and come work for me in Florida. All you have to do is ask! You know the family will always find you a proper job and we would love to see more of you. Four hotels mean lots of cafes and restaurants, and they all need great chefs and managers like you."

Then she smiled and winked. "Think about our lovely beaches and all of those handsome surfers. You would love it here."

Lottie lifted her phone so that the lens was pointing out towards the neat thatched cottages that lined the narrow road that led toward Kingsmede. A patchwork of small fields and copses of bright green trees on the rolling chalk hills was a perfect backdrop in the warm June sunshine.

"The view is not too bad here either Mum," Lottie laughed and turned the phone around to face her. "Not too many surfers around in this part of Hampshire, I'll give you

Even Page Footer -Section 2-

2

19

FORMATTING THE BODY TEXT OF YOUR BOOK

If you formatted your document as described in the opening chapters when we created a very clean version of your text, then you should be starting from a great position which makes it very easy to polish the main body of your novel.

The Body of Your Novel

Each new chapter will have a chapter title and will start on a new page. Then the body text of your novel follows within each chapter.

If you have a very long book, then you can use Parts to divide sections of the book and start each part on a new page.

In chapter four we customised and set the "Normal" style for your body text, including font and font size, page alignment and how to insert a first line paragraph indent.

In chapter five we discussed how to customise the format and customise the "Header 1 "style for all of the chapter headings so that they are consistent throughout your novel. If you have not already done so, click on the chapter title and change the style to Heading 1.

These two styles – Normal and Header 1 determine the core appearance of your novel.

In this chapter we are going to cover:

#A. Line spacing.

#B. Styling the first paragraph of new chapter, including how to change the first letter into a dropped cap.

#C. How to use scene separators within a chapter.

#A. Line Spacing

This is an example from page one of chapter one from the working draft of the case study novel. The chapter title has already been formatted but the body text is currently set to **Normal** style which is left-aligned and single-spaced text in Merriweather 10 point. The paragraph indent is set to 0.3. **Time to make this body text sparkle!**

Step One. Line Spacing. To adjust line spacing between the rows of text.

The current text is single spaced. This is fine for Kindle eBooks but for print books it is best to increase the line spacing slightly so that it is easier to read.

To adjust the line spacing in Word.

1. Select **all the paragraphs of text** on the first page of the chapter.

2. Click into the **Home tab** in the header bar. Then **Paragraph**.

3. Under **Line Spacing select Multiple** then type in **1.3**. Then **OK**.

This sets the paragraph line spacing to 1.3 lines. Take a look at the impact this line spacing makes in your novel and increase the spacing as needed.

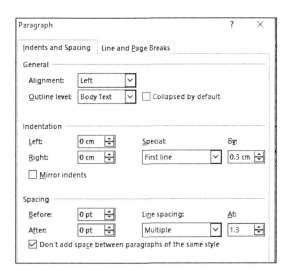

Here is an example for the same text with line spacing at 1.2 and then at 1.3.

Chapter One

Lottie Brannigan took a deep breath, picked up her phone and smiled at the tiny screen showing a live video of her mother, who was standing in a large windowless meeting room with a clipboard in her hand.

Isabella Russo was wearing a low-cut cream silk blouse, caramel slacks, and her best Florida tan. She looked every inch the professional hotel manager and business woman.

A tinny and very English female voice boomed out and bounced around the inside of the cab of Lottie's delivery van, making her ears rattle. "Sorry about the speaker phone, cara, I'm just about to brief the team about today's conference schedule. I just wanted to call and wish you a very happy birthday. It's not every day that my baby girl turns twenty-eight. You look marvelous, darling."

Then her mother's voice faded away and her fingers flicked towards the screen. "Although, that pony tail really does not work with your thick hair and you need to do something about those shadows under your eyes. When are you going to start going out and looking pretty again?"

Chapter One

Lottie Brannigan took a deep breath, picked up her phone and smiled at the tiny screen showing a live video of her mother, who was standing in a large windowless meeting room with a clipboard in her hand.

Isabella Russo was wearing a low-cut cream silk blouse, caramel slacks, and her best Florida tan. She looked every inch the professional hotel manager and business woman.

A tinny and very English female voice boomed out and bounced around the inside of the cab of Lottie's delivery van, making her ears rattle. "Sorry about the speaker phone, cara, I'm just about to brief the team about today's conference schedule. I just wanted to call and wish you a very happy birthday. It's not every day that my baby girl turns twenty-eight. You look marvelous, darling."

Then her mother's voice faded away and her fingers flicked towards the screen. "Although, that pony tail really does not work with your thick hair and you need to do something about those shadows under

Which one do you think looks better? Save your document – but don't change any of the styles until you have complete Step Two.

To adjust the line spacing in Google Docs.

1. Select **all the paragraphs of text** on the first page of the chapter.

2. Click into the **Format tab** in the header bar in **Editing Mode**. Then **Line Spacing**.

3. Under **Line Spacing select Custom Spacing** then type in **1.3**. Then **Apply.**

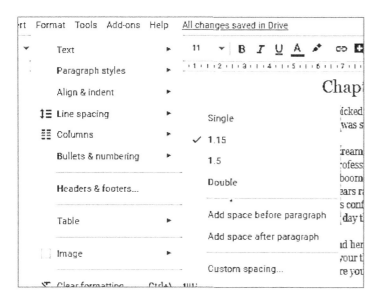

Step Two. Line Spacing. To add space between the paragraphs.

This creates a tiny break between the paragraphs which makes a novel and other text-heavy books very much easier to read.

To adjust the line spacing between paragraphs in Word.

1. Select **all the paragraphs of text** on the first page of the chapter.

2. Click into the **Home tab** in the header bar. Then **Paragraph**.

3. Unclick the box that says "Don't add space between paragraphs of the same style".

4. Under **Spacing select After** then type in **3**. Then **OK**.

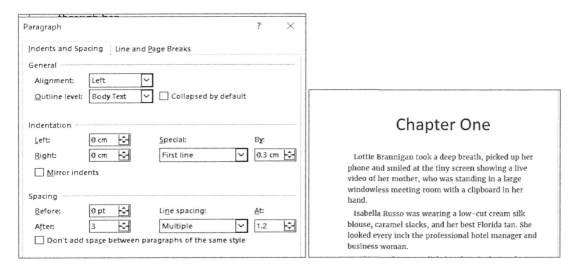

This inserts a 3-point space between paragraphs. For most novels this space works well but you can, of course, reduce or increase the space for your specific work.

In Google Docs.

Repeat the previous steps used to set line spacing. **Format. Line Spacing. Custom Spacing.** Then set **Paragraph Spacing After** to the number you want and click **Apply.**

Creating a Body Text Style for Your Novel

When you have customised your text to look precisely how you want it, it is often a good idea to save that specific combination of style elements in a new text style.

To create a new style in Word.

1. Select **all the paragraphs of text** on the first page of the chapter which you have just updated with line and paragraph spacing.

2. **Right click on your mouse** and then click on **Styles**.

3. A pop-up box should appear with all of the styles that you are using for your document. At the moment the style is still Normal. Go to the bottom of the box and **Create a Style.**

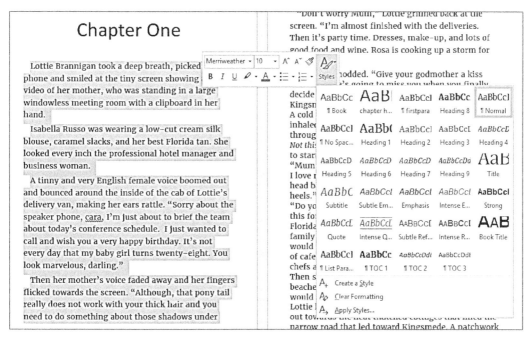

4. **OR go to the Home tab and then Styles. Click on the down pointing arrow with a bar on top in the right scroll bar. This brings up more style options.**

Click on Create a Style.

5. **Give this new style a name, such as Script, or something similar, to indicate that this style is only for the body text. Then Click OK.**

6. The style called Script, or your chosen name, will now be listed in the Styles options in the header bar under Styles.

7. Select all of the text in the rest of the chapter and apply the style to that text by clicking on the new style name.

8. Review what your new text style looks like when applied to a complete chapter.

9. If you like the style, go through every one of the chapters in your novel.

   Select all of the text of that chapter, excluding the chapter title of course, and apply that style to all of the text by clicking on the new style name.
   Tip. To make it easier to select text from a complete chapter, reduce the zoom on your page view so that you can see multiple pages at the same time.

10. If you don't like it and want to change it, click on the style name and use the Modify option to edit this new style. You can do this at any time and all of the text where this style has been used will be updated with the new features.

In Google Docs.

When you have set the body text to the exact line spacing and paragraph spacing that you want, save it as the default Normal style.

1. Highlight a few paragraphs of formatted text.

2. Then go to the **Style tab** in the header.

3. Click on **Normal** then **Update Normal text to match.**

#B. Styling the first paragraph of each new chapter, including how to change the first letter into a dropped cap.

#1. By convention the first line of the first paragraph of any new chapter is not indented. In addition;

#2. The first letter of the first word of the first sentence of the first paragraph is often "dropped" as a large capital letter. This is completely optional, but many authors still prefer to use a dropped cap. The alternative is to change the first few words in the first sentence into upper case capital letters to distinguish them from the remainder of the chapter. Use of first letter dropped caps is very much a personal choice and many commercial publishers no longer use this style.

#1. How to Remove the Indent on the first line of the first paragraph of any new chapter in Word.

1. Select **the first paragraphs of text** in chapter one.

2. Click into the **Home tab** in the header bar. Then **Paragraph**.

3. In the **Special** Setting, use the drop-down chevron to change the setting from First Line to **None**. Then **OK**.

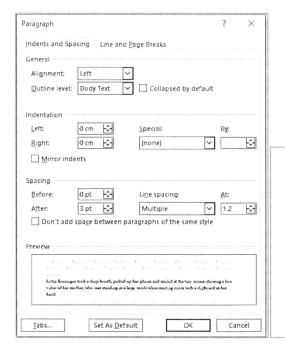

Chapter One

Lottie Brannigan took a deep breath, picked up her phone and smiled at the tiny screen showing a live video of her mother, who was standing in a large windowless meeting room with a clipboard in her hand.

Isabella Russo was wearing a low-cut cream silk blouse, caramel slacks, and her best Florida tan. She looked every inch the professional hotel manager and business woman.

This removes the indent from just that first paragraph that you have selected.

You can now Repeat this Step for the first paragraph in every chapter of your novel.

Or You can Create a New Style in exactly the same way as we have just gone through for the body text, by highlighting this newly formatted first paragraph and calling it **First Paragraph Style or similar.** You can then apply that new First Paragraph style to the first paragraph of every chapter in your novel.

In Google Docs.

1. Select the first paragraph of chapter one.

2. Go to the **Format Tab** in the header bar in **Editing** Mode. Then **Align and Indent.**

3. Then **Indentation Options.**

4. Select **None** to remove the indent for this paragraph.

5. You will have to repeat this step manually for the first paragraph of each chapter. There is no first paragraph style option.

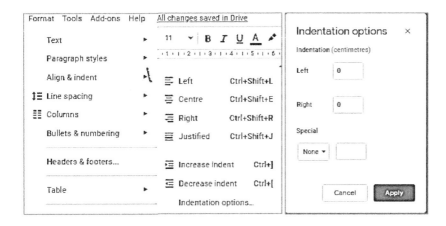

#2. How to Insert a "Dropped" capital letter.

In Word.

1. **Select the first letter of the first word of the first sentence of the first paragraph of the first chapter.**

2. **Click into the Insert Tab in the header bar. Then the Text menu.**

3. **Click on Dropped.**

4. This will then insert a capital of the letter that you have selected and drop it 3 lines down in the paragraph and no distance at all from the next letter in that sentence. Personally, I find 3 lines is too large for a commercial novel in a medium trim size.

5. **Click on Drop Cap Options.** This allows you to change the font of the first letter, the number of lines the letter will drop and the gap to the next letter in the sentence. I would recommend changing the Lines to Drop to 2 but leaving the gap as 0cm. See the examples below for how this looks in the case study.

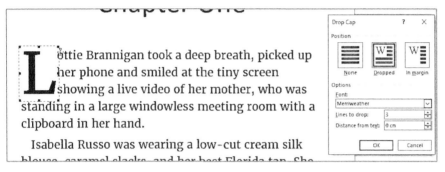

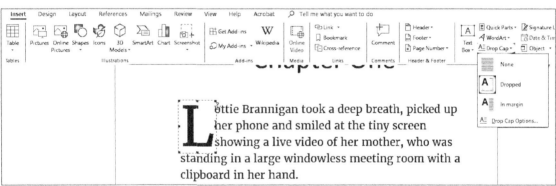

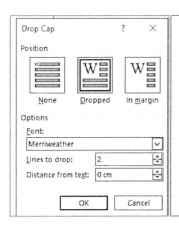

Chapter One

Lottie Brannigan took a deep breath, picked up her phone and smiled at the tiny screen showing a live video of her mother, who was standing in a large windowless meeting room with a clipboard in her hand.

Isabella Russo was wearing a low-cut cream silk blouse, caramel slacks, and her best Florida tan. She looked every inch the professional hotel manager and business woman.

In Google Docs.

There is no option to format the first letter as a dropped cap to the best of my knowledge. Some authors prefer to use an alternative style and change the first few words of the opening paragraph of every new chapter to Uppercase.

1. Select the first few words in the opening paragraph of chapter one.

2. Go to the **Format tab** in the header in Editing Mode. Then **Text** then **Capitalisation**.

3. Select **Upper Case** for the selected text.

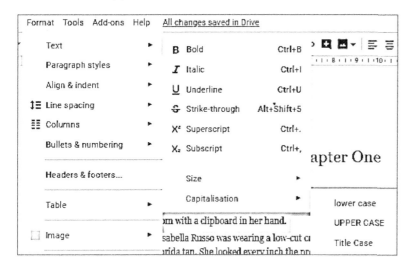

Chapter One

LOTTIE BRANNIGAN TOOK A DEEP BREATH, picked up her phone and smiled at the tiny screen showing a live video of her mother, who was standing in a large windowless meeting room with a clipboard in her hand.

4. **Repeat this step** for the opening paragraph of every new chapter in your novel.

#C. How to use scene separators within a chapter.
Inserting a Scene Separator Symbol or Image

Many authors use 3 asterisks *** or other text symbols to indicate when a scene ends within a chapter. You can also use a decorative font such as Grand Vibes or Webdings to insert more decorative letters. Be sure to add a spacing before and after of at least 6 point to separate the scenes.

"Oh Lord, she's going." Prisha waved frantically at Rosa while waving a chunk of bruschetta. "Quick. We need champagne and we need it now. Time to get this party started!"

∞ ∞ ∞

Two hours later the main course plates had been cleared away, the party was in full flow and Toby was topping up the glasses with the excellent Chianti which was his birthday present to Lottie.

Grand Vibes 16

"Oh Lord, she's going." Prisha waved frantically at Rosa while waving a chunk of bruschetta. "Quick. We need champagne and we need it now. Time to get this party started!"

✢ ✢ ✢

Two hours later the main course plates had been cleared away, the party was in full flow and Toby was topping up the glasses with the excellent Chianti which was his birthday present to Lottie.

Webdings 14

If you want to use an image, use the **Insert Tab** and then **Pictures.**

OR in Google Docs. Use Insert Image.

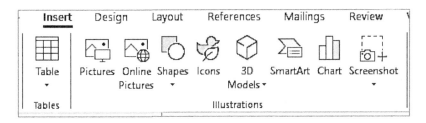

"Oh Lord, she's going." Prisha waved frantically at Rosa while waving a chunk of bruschetta. "Quick. We need champagne and we need it now. Time to get this party started!"

Two hours later the main course plates had been cleared away, the party was in full flow and Toby was topping up the glasses with the excellent Chianti which was his birthday present to Lottie.

You can purchase stock images of decorative scrolls and genre-relevant artwork very cheaply from stock image sites. Always reduce the size of the image so that it does not distract from the content of the novel.

WIDOWS AND ORPHANS

Traditionally, one of the roles of a proofreader was to check that the text of the book was easy to read and looked attractive to the reader.

Two of the conventions that are still used by professional printers are that single lines of text should not appear alone at the top or the bottom of a printed page. These split-paragraphs or single sentences are also known as **widows and orphans**.

A **Widow** is when the last line of a paragraph falls <u>at the top</u> of a new page or column.

An **Orphan** describes the first line of a new paragraph that falls <u>on the bottom</u> of a page or column.

These conventions are not strictly followed for non-fiction books, but in fiction, a single line of text from a paragraph standing alone at the bottom or top of a page can distract the reader and pull them out of the story they are enjoying. It also breaks the balance of a printed book.

How to Correct Text Spacing to Avoid Split Paragraphs

The basic technique is to edit the spacing of the text on that page to either insert or remove a line of text so that the single, stand-alone, line of text is reunited with the parent paragraph.

A Widow Split-Paragraph or Single Line of Text

If the last line of a paragraph falls at the top of a new page or column, you can edit the text in the previous paragraphs to **remove a line space** or a line of text so that the widow line is pulled back to the previous page and the main paragraph it came from.

This is a particular problem if this is the last line of a chapter or dedication etc. and the rest of the page would otherwise be blank.

There are several ways of doing this:

• Set your word processing software to automatically control Widows and Orphans.

In Word, you can apply this to the entire document or the single chapter that you are having problems with. Select the text, then go to Paragraph formatting under the Home menu tab and click on the Widow/Orphan control option.

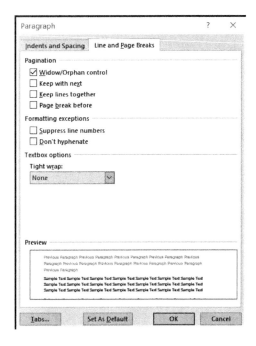

• Remove a paragraph break so that you take out a line break between the paragraphs. This closes up the text and pulls the last line back into the last paragraph.

• Rewrite the text if you are the author. You can usually edit out enough words to remove one line of text.

• If you cannot edit the text, you can also use Character Spacing to tighten the space between characters in one or more previous paragraphs. If this is used carefully, it will be invisible to the reader.

In Word.

1. Select the text, then go to Font formatting under the Home menu tab.

2. Click on the Advanced tab, then the Character Spacing option.

3. In the Spacing box, choose **Condensed**. In the By box, click the down arrow to "0.1 pt" appears. Click OK, then review the position of the Widow text.

If you need to remove more space, try 0.2 pt. Any more than that, and the condensing looks obvious.

An Orphan Split-Paragraph.

If the first line of a new paragraph falls on the bottom of a page or column, you can follow the same approach used to correct for a Widow, but in this case you edit the text in the previous paragraphs to **add an extra line space** or a line of text so that the Orphan line is pushed onto the next page and re-joins the rest of the parent paragraph.

You therefore reverse the instructions used for the Widow control to add space.

• Set your word processing software to automatically control Widows and Orphans as just described.

• Add a paragraph break in a block of text if you can, so that you insert a line break between the paragraphs. This pushes down the text and moves the last line back onto the next page.

• Rewrite the text if you are the author. You can usually add enough words to create one line of text.

• If you cannot edit the text, you can also use Character Spacing to expand the spacing between characters in one of more previous paragraphs by one line.

If this is used carefully, it will be invisible to the reader.

In Word.

1. Select the text, then go to Font formatting under the Home menu tab.

2. Click on the Advanced tab, then the Character Spacing option.

3. In the Spacing box, choose **Expanded**. In the By box, click the down arrow to "0.1 pt" appears. Click OK, then check that the Orphan text has moved onto the next page.

If you need to add more space, try 0.2 pt. Any more than that, and the expanded text may look obvious to the reader.

These professional touches will enhance the reading experience of your work without altering too much of your content or being obtrusive.

Chapter Formatting Checklist

√   **Formatted and Customised the Chapter Title**

√   **Created a New Style for the Body Text**

√   •   Alignment of the Text

√   •   Font and Font Size

√   •   First Line Paragraph Indent

√   •   Line Spacing in the Text

√   •   Line Spacing between Paragraphs

√   **Inserted a Scene Separator**

√   **Created a New Style for the First Paragraph of Each New Chapter**

√   •   No Indent in the First Paragraph

√   •   Learnt how to Set a Dropped Cap for the First Letter

√   •   Learnt how to Correct Split Paragraphs

20

FORMATTING THE BACK MATTER OF YOUR BOOK

The Back-matter content is the information in the back of the book, found in the pages after the main text of the novel.

Most marketing-savvy indie fiction authors utilize back matter to:

#invite readers to join their mailing list,

#give extra details about the book and themselves, and, most importantly,

#give a preview extract of the next book in a series to help convince readers who have just enjoyed this novel to buy the next book or another book by the same author. This could always be a backlist book if you don't have the next book in the series available or on pre-order.

The idea is simple. Use the back-matter content to drive people to buy or per-order your next book and/or join your mailing list.

What does the back matter of a print book look like for modern indie authors?
The back matter of a printed indie novel will typically follow this sequence:

- **Any acknowledgements.** (Optional)

- **A list of other books from the author.**

- **An exclusive extract from the next book in the series or another similar book.** (Optional but highly recommended)

- **Note from the author**, thanking the reader for buying the book and asking them to leave a review on the online store where they bought the book.

- **Offer a free reader magnet** if the reader subscribes to your mailing list.

- **About the Author page** with links to your website and social media profile pages, where they will be more opportunities to take the reader away from Amazon and onto your mailing list. You can add an author photo here if you wish

Worked Examples from Case Study One. A Short Mystery Novel

You will note that:

- This is the first book in a new cozy mystery series, and I wanted the readers to recognise that the second book was already written and available. Readers love series and prefer to invest their time in a book where others in the series are available. There is a sample of the beginning of book two at the end of this book.

- I always thank readers and ask them to leave a review of the book.

- I offer free books and bonuses to my mailing list subscribers through the Sophie Brent website.

Page Numbering in the Back Matter

The back matter follows on with the same page numbering as the main text, so you don't have any special page number formatting to worry about.

Page Headings in the Back Matter

Think about which pages you want to include in the table of contents for your book.

As a minimum I would include the **Acknowledgements page and the About the Author page**. For these pages you would format the heading using the Heading 1 style.

There is no need to remove the headers and footers or page numbers from the back-matter pages, but you can do so if you wish by inserting Section Break/Next Page at the start of each page and then deleting a few lines to break up the start of the text for that new section.

THANK YOU!

Thank you for reading **Murder and Mozzarella!**
I hope that you enjoyed this first book in a new series
set in the Hampshire village of Kingsmede. I love
sharing this special world and the people who live
there with cozy mystery readers.
If you enjoyed this story, I would really appreciate it
if you would consider leaving a review of this book,
no matter how short, at the retailer site where you
bought your copy or on sites like Goodreads.
YOU are the key to this book's success.
I read every review and they really do make a huge
difference.
Reviews help other readers to discover the kind of
stories they want to read and are a great way to
support authors.

If you would like to find out what Lottie and her pals
get up to next, the second book in the Kingsmede
Cozy Mystery Series, **MURDER AND MERLOT** is **OUT
NOW!**

Turn the page **now** to read the first chapter for free.

*OTHER BOOKS IN THE
KINGSMEDE COZY MYSTERY
SERIES.*

MURDER AND MOZZARELLA (Book 1) – __OUT NOW!__
MURDER AND MERLOT (Book 2) – __OUT NOW!__
MURDER AND MORELLO (Book 3) –ON PRE–ORDER

WOULD YOU LIKE TO RECEIVE *FREE* COPIES OF
FUTURE BOOKS BY SOPHIE BRENT, EXCLUSIVE
NEWS AND GIVEAWAYS?

CLICK BELOW TO JOIN THE SOPHIE BRENT
READER GROUP!

SophieBrent.com

Page Layout in the Back Matter

Some authors prefer to have the key pages, such as the About the Author page, on a right-hand, odd-numbered page in their print book, even if this means having to insert a blank page. If you wish to do this, follow the same process that we used in the front matter and use Section Break/Next Page to insert a blank page.

21

CREATING A TABLE OF CONTENTS

Automatic Table of Contents for Print Books

The simplest and fastest way to create a Table of Contents for your print book is to use the software to generate one for you. You can be confident that the page numbers will always be correct and if you make changes to the text, it takes seconds to update the contents.

In Word.

1. Open your document. Go to the page in the front matter where you have a page with the title Contents.
2. Go to the **References tab** in the header bar.
3. Click on **Table of Contents.** Then use the down arrow to select **Custom Table of Contents option** at the bottom of the box.

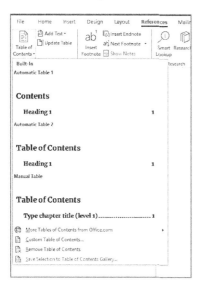

4. **Check "Show Page Numbers".**

Uncheck "Use hyperlinks instead of page numbers".
General. Show levels – change this to 1 (which will be Heading 1) unless your novel is divided into parts, in which case change this to 2.

5. **Go to Options. Scroll down** all the styles that you can use to build a Table of Contents. **Select Heading 1** and delete the (1) number against any other style that may be listed as an option.

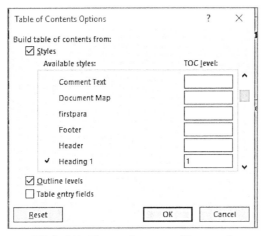

6. **Click OK.** The software will now detect all Heading 1 text and list that text with the page number associated with it in your document.

Modifying the Table of Contents Style

If you prefer to have dotted lines between the title and the page number or other styling, then you can use Word to modify this for you automatically.

In Word.

1. Open your document. Click on the Table of Contents you have just created.

2. Go to the **References tab** in the header bar.

3. Click on **Table of Contents.** Then use the down arrow to select **Custom Table of Contents option** at the bottom of the box.

4. Click on **From Template.** Then use the **Preview to** see what each template looks like. Select a new template for your contents.

Examples from the case study novel. The Classic and Formal Templates.

CONTENTS		CONTENTS	
Chapter One	1	CHAPTER ONE	1
Chapter Two	12	CHAPTER TWO	12
Chapter Three	23	CHAPTER THREE	23
Chapter Four	41	CHAPTER FOUR	41
Chapter Five	51	CHAPTER FIVE	51
Chapter Six	65	CHAPTER SIX	65
Chapter Seven	76	CHAPTER SEVEN	76
Chapter Eight	93	CHAPTER EIGHT	93
Chapter Nine	102	CHAPTER NINE	102
Chapter Ten	112	CHAPTER TEN	112
Chapter Eleven	124	CHAPTER ELEVEN	124
Chapter Twelve	134	CHAPTER TWELVE	134
Chapter Thirteen	150	CHAPTER THIRTEEN	150
Chapter Fourteen	161	CHAPTER FOURTEEN	161
Chapter Fifteen	171	CHAPTER FIFTEEN	171
Chapter Sixteen	181	CHAPTER SIXTEEN	181
Chapter Seventeen	190	CHAPTER SEVENTEEN	190
Chapter Eighteen	200	CHAPTER EIGHTEEN	200
THANK YOU!	207	THANK YOU!	207
ABOUT MURDER AND MERLOT	208	ABOUT MURDER AND MERLOT	208
ABOUT THE AUTHOR	216	CHAPTER ONE	209
		ABOUT THE AUTHOR	216

5. **To change the font and font size used, select the Modify Option.** This will take you to the font option menu and you can select any font combination that you wish.

To update the table of contents at any time, simply click on the table and right click if you are using a mouse. Then click on **Update Field**.

If you had added text but not added new chapter headings/Header 1 pages, then **click on Update Page Numbers Only**. Otherwise **Update Entire Table.**

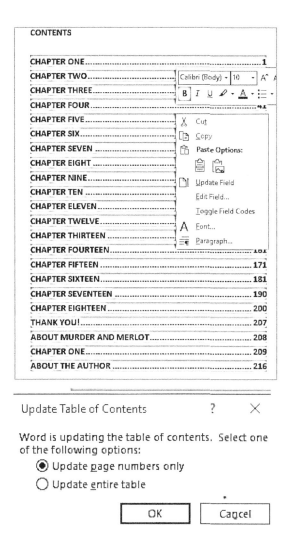

CONTENTS

Update Table of Contents ? ✕

Word is updating the table of contents. Select one of the following options:

◉ Update page numbers only
◯ Update entire table

OK   Cancel

Inserting a Table of Contents in Google Docs.

1. Place your cursor in the position where you want the Table of Contents.

2. Go to **Insert** in the **Editing** mode, then **Table of Contents.**

3. **Select the option** which will show page numbers. [Hyperlinks are for eBooks]

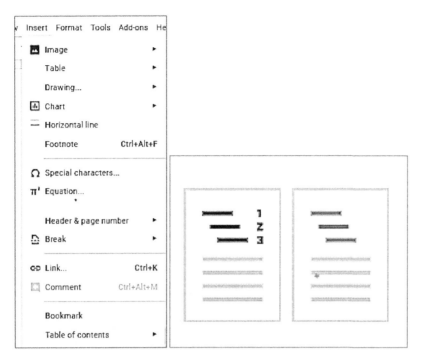

4. Change the font and font size of the entries by selecting the entire table of contents then clicking on the font options in the header.

5. You can expand the text of each chapter title by clicking the text and changing the entry for that line.

For both Word and Google Docs.

The alternative to inserting an automatic Table of Contents is to manually create a table and type in the chapter headings and the page numbers from the final draft of your novel. This can be time consuming, but it does allow some authors the creativity they are looking for, especially if you want different layouts with images and graphic design elements.

Use **Insert Table.** Then Insert 2 columns and as many rows as there are chapters plus one.

Type, or copy and paste, the name of the chapter into column one and the page number for that chapter into column two. You can then format the font, font size and alignment and add custom text.

Remove all of the gridlines and borders from the table when you have finished.

22

SAVING YOUR FORMATTED BOOK INTERIOR AS A PDF

Once you are completely happy with your print book, you can move on to saving the book interior as a print-ready PDF which you can upload onto KDP.

Step One. Save your Word or text document as FINAL.

Step Two. Save your document as a PDF.

In Word.

1. Open the document.

2. Click on **Save As** in the **File Menu.**

3. Select **PDF** from the list of file formats.

4. Click **More Options**. Check that PDF/A is ticked.

5. Click **Tools** in the bottom left of the screen. Then **Save Options. And Embed Fonts in this file.**

   Make sure that all the following options are checked or ticked:
   - Fonts and images are embedded.

   - Bookmarks, annotations, and comments are disabled.

   - PDF/X format is used if possible. Otherwise PDF/A Compliant.

6. **Give your PDF a name and save the PDF** in the folder for your book. Then **OK.**

7. Open the PDF and go through every page to make sure that it still looks the way you want it – this is what your reader will see. Any problems? Change the Word document and resave as a PDF.

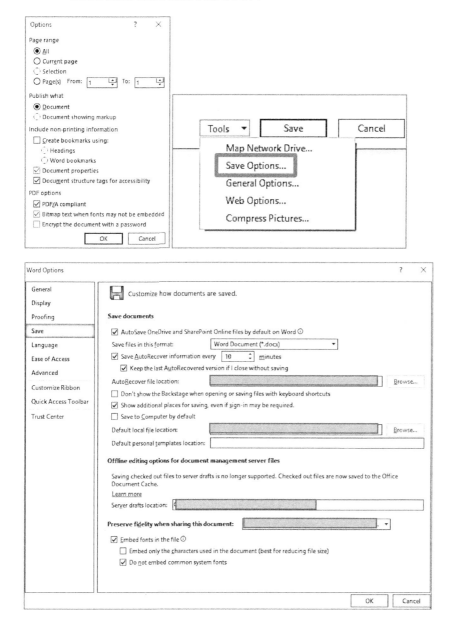

In Google Docs.

Open Document and in the File Tab select Download as PDF document.

Google Docs.

To the best of my knowledge it is not possible to export a print-ready PDF from Google docs. I am not aware of any way to embed fonts in the PDF or save as a PDF/A or PDF/X.

I would recommend using another software program to convert this PDF into a format that KDP print would accept or exporting your document into another file format such as MS Word (.docx).

23

BOOK COVER LAYOUT FOR PRINT BOOKS

If you have already created a Kindle eBook version of your novel, then you know that KDP expects you to submit the eBook cover as a single image in Jpeg format. This is because, essentially, the eBook cover represents the front cover.

Print book covers are completely different.

You will need to have artwork for the front cover, the spine if there are enough pages in your novel to create one, and the back cover of your book. KDP and other print on demand publishers ask for the complete book cover to be uploaded as one complete continuous image centred left to right on the spine as a PDF file.

The complete cover design will therefore be made up of three parts:

The back cover, the spine of your book, and the front cover.

In addition, you need to include extra space around the outer edge of the book, called the Bleed, which is where the paper will be trimmed during the printing process.

Amazon KDP specifies a minimum standard bleed of 0.125" (3 mm) for all print books and this needs to be added to the width and height dimensions of your cover PDF.

Creating a Print-Ready Paperback Cover

In chapter four of this book we covered the many options available to independently published authors. Investing time and money in a great cover design is one of the best things you can do to market your book, no matter what genre it fits into.

Book cover design is a very complex process and outside the scope of this book, but KDP Print does provides some free tools to help the indie author to format and lay out their design as a paperback book cover.

The KDP Cover Creator

This is a free tool that helps you design your own eBook and paperback cover.

You can download and explore this tool and experiment to see if it is a good fit for your novel from the KDP website. **https://kdp.amazon.com/en_US/help/topic/G201113520**

KDP Cover Templates

KDP provides a very useful template that you can download with the correct cover dimensions for your specific combination of page count, trim size and paper. All of the dimensions for your book will be embedded in the template.

https://kdp.amazon.com/en_US/cover-templates

The template can be downloaded as a zip file with a PDF and a .png image.

Example. For our 6" x 9" novel with 200 printed pages on **White Paper**

The Black Dotted line is the final trim size where the paper will be cut to size.

The White Area is the live area where you can place your cover images and text.

The Red Area is out of bounds for text or essential images. The background colour and artwork must fill the red area since it will be part of your printed book. The spine text has to be placed well within the red area boundaries. The width of the red area is a good indication of the variability in the printing and binding process.

The Yellow Barcode is always printed in the same place on the back cover, so this area is out of bounds for text or images.

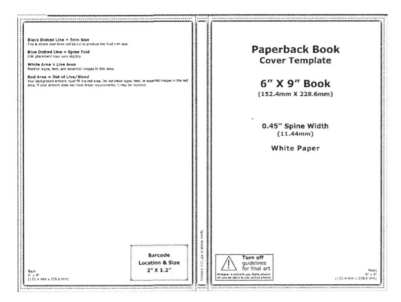

How to Use the Cover Templates

Select the graphic design software packages that you are familiar with, such as **Microsoft Word, PowerPoint presentations, Canva (free), Keynote presentations, GIMP (free), Photoshop or similar.**

If you are happy to create the layout for your own paperback cover then here are some essential guidelines to get you started.

The one variable dimension in any print cover design is the width of the spine, since this is totally dependent on the number of pages in your novel, so let's start there.

Calculating the Width of the Spine of your book

The width of the spine is determined by the final number of pages for that trim size of your novel. The more pages in your book, then the thicker the book spine will be for a set trim size.

This is crucial. You should always wait until the novel is finished, the trim size is fixed and all the formatting has been completed, before designing your print book cover, or ordering a design.

The cover designer needs to have the width of the spine before they can finish the design for the full combined spread of your complete paperback cover.

Calculating the Spine measurements for your novel.

The spine measurement can be calculated as follows:

- White paper: page count x 0.002252" (0.0572 mm)

- Cream paper: page count x 0.0025" (0.0635 mm)

In addition, because the spine position may vary very slightly during the binding and publishing process, KDP print requires that you allow **for an extra space of 0.0625" (1.6 mm) variance space between the text and the edge of the spine on either side of the spine where the cover will be folded over.**

The Total Spine Width = Space + Spine Measurement + Space.

Example. A novel with **200 printed pages** on **White Paper** would have the following spine width.

Required Extra Spine space	0.0625" (1.6 mm)
White Paper and Black Ink: 200 x 0.002252" (0.0572 mm)	0.45" (11.44 mm)
Required Extra Spine space	0.0625" (1.6 mm)
Total Spine Width for your print book cover design	0.575 inches (14.64mm)

Example. A novel with **200 printed pages** on **Cream Paper** would have the following spine width. This would be larger than the white paper because cream paper is thicker.

Required Extra Spine space	0.0625" (1.6 mm)
White Paper and Black Ink: 200 x 0.0025" (0.0635 mm)	0.50" (12.7 mm)
Required Extra Spine space	0.0625" (1.6 mm)
Total Spine Width for your print book cover design	0.625 inches (15.9 mm)

Calculating the Overall Cover Dimensions

The Total Cover Width = Bleed + Back Cover Width + Spine Width + Front Cover Width + Bleed.

Example. Imagine the trim size for your novel is 6" x 9" and it has **200 printed pages** on **White Paper**

Left Outside Bleed	0.125" (3 mm)
Back cover width	6" (152.4 mm)
Spine width	0.575 "(14.64 mm)
Front Cover width	6" (152.4 mm)
Right Outside Bleed	0.125" (3 mm)
Total Combined Width	**12.824" (325.4 mm)**

The Total Cover Height = Bleed + Trim Height + Bleed.

Example. Imagine the trim size for your novel is 6" x 9"

Top Outside Bleed	0.125" (3 mm)
The back cover, spine and front cover are the same height	9" (228.6 mm)
Bottom Outside Bleed	0.125" (3 mm)
Total Combined Height	**9.25" (234.6 mm)**

Applying the Cover Template

Once you know the exact cover dimensions, create a new file using the custom dimensions of your paperback book cover that you have just calculated.

Upload the image of the template book cover from KDP and paste it onto the new file shape that you have created.

You can either use it, for example, as a guide using layers in your software, or make it more transparent and add images and text over the base layer.

This will vary between the various software packages, but your final design should be of the correct dimensions and meet all of KDP print requirements for spacing.

If you are using a cover designer, they will ask you for the trim size and the number of pages in your book so that they can make this calculation for you.

When you have added the content to the front, spine and back cover of your design, then save and export the complete design as a print-ready PDF. Be sure to check that the fonts are embedded, and the image layers have been flattened.

When you upload the PDF of your book cover onto KDP the cover will be linked to the text PDF of your book and you can check the precise layout of the cover design in the Book Previewer.

Here is an example from the case study, taken from the print preview screen. I could have made the spine text smaller, but this simple layout was accepted by KDP.

One advantage of designing your own print covers is that, if there any problems reported by Amazon during review, it only takes a few minutes to correct the cover, save a new PDF and upload it onto KDP.

It is also very useful if you are planning a series linked books. For example.

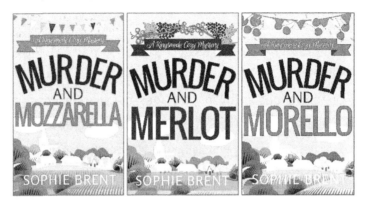

More information on print book cover design and layout for KDP Print can be found on the KDP website and I would encourage you to make yourself very familiar with the specifications required.

https://kdp.amazon.com/en_US/help/topic/G201857950#coverspec

https://kdp.amazon.com/en_US/help/topic/G201953020

https://kdp.amazon.com/en_US/help/topic/G201113520

KDP will reject your print book during quality review if the book cover dimensions are not a perfect fit for your specified trim size, or the spine text is too large for the spine width.

24

PUBLISHING A KDP PRINT PAPERBACK BOOK

YOUR KINDLE DIRECT PUBLISHING ACCOUNT

If you don't already have a KDP account, follow the instructions on the home page to set-up your account and payment details. For example. https://kdp.amazon.com/en_US/

Note: If you are completely new to KDP, then I recommend that you click on Getting Started tips, where you will find a full range of written instructions and video tutorials on how to use the platform to self-publish your work.

You will be taken to a Bookshelf page where you can **Create a New title**.

Click on the + Paperback box

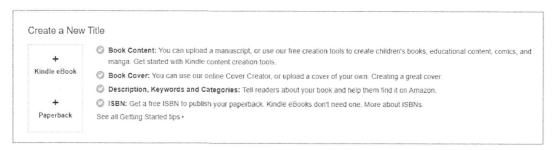

You will be taken to the **Paperback Set-up pages.**

If you don't have a Kindle eBook set-up already, it only takes a few minutes to complete the data for your paperback.

Paperback Book Details Page

Start working down the page, completing each section in turn until you have a complete profile for your paperback book.

You will find detailed instructions on how to complete the Book Details in chapter three of this book. Be sure to pay attention to the Keywords and Category selections for your book.

Be sure to click *Save as Draft* or *Save and Continue* before leaving this page.

Paperback Content Page

Murder and Mozzarella

Paperback Details	Paperback Content	Paperback Rights & Pricing
✓ Complete	*i* In Progress...	*i* Not Started...

Print ISBN To comply with industry standards, all paperbacks are required to have a unique ISBN. What is an ISBN? ▾

⦿ Get a free KDP ISBN

Assign me a free KDP ISBN

◯ Use my own ISBN

Publication Date Enter the date on which your book was first published. Leave this blank if you are publishing your book for the first time. How is my book's publication date determined? ▾

Publication Date (Optional)

Your 'Live on Amazon' date will be used

The KDP ISBN.

We covered this in detail in chapter three. An ISBN is required for all print books. Amazon can provide a free ISBN, but they will be recorded as the publisher.

This is the place to add your own ISBN if you have purchased a bundle and wish to be add your own publisher name.

Print ISBN To comply with industry standards, all paperbacks are required to have a unique ISBN. What is an ISBN? ▾

⦿ Get a free KDP ISBN

Assign me a free KDP ISBN ✓ Your book has been assigned a free KDP ISBN:
ISBN: 9781795824910
Imprint: Independently published

◯ Use my own ISBN

Publication Date. Leave this blank if you are publishing your book for the first time.

Print Options.

Interior & paper type. Do you prefer white or cream paper for your book?

Trim Size. This is where you set the dimensions of the paperback version of your book. For clarification – this is the finished height and width of the completed book as you are holding it.

The Bleed Settings. This is where you include images which extend beyond the print margins to the edge of the book cover. This does not normally apply for novels but may apply to the covers of non-fiction books.

Paperback cover finish. Selecting a matte or a glossy cover for your paperback is a personal choice. Most novels have matte covers which do not show finger marks so easily.

Manuscript

Upload the PDF of your formatted book interior.

It will take a few minutes for the system to process your manuscript.

Paperback Book Cover

Upload the print-ready PDF of your paperback book cover.

It will take a few minutes for the system to process your book cover file.

Remember this is the full cover "flat" PDF of your entire book, including the back cover, the spine text and the front cover, together with a working margin around the entire graphic design.

For example.

Once the book interior PDF and the book cover PDF have been loaded, the KDP system with link the two files together to create your paperback book.

25

USING THE KDP PRINT PREVIEWER TOOL

Book Preview

Just as with your Kindle eBook, it is essential that you use the online Book Preview facility to check that your paperback looks the way that you want it.

Book Preview	Preview your file to check for formatting and print quality issues. Learn more about formatting and print quality on KDP.
	Launch Previewer

Click on Launch Print Previewer.

It can take a few minutes for the system to link the book cover and contents to create a print-ready file.

What you will see will be a "spread" of your print book in a two-page layout, starting with the combined full book cover.

Most of the quality issues indie authors see with print on demand paperbacks are associated with the cover design rather than the content of the novel.

Dotted lines on the cover of your proof indicate the strict limits on where you can place text. Because of variability in the printing process, you must allow for extra space around the text on the spine on your book and along every edge of the book cover.

Your book cover will be rejected if the text goes over the dotted lines. This can be a particular problem if the width of the spine is very narrow and you are squeezing the title into a small space.

The bar code with the ISBN will be printed in the same location every time – the bottom right corner of the book.

Your book will be rejected if the text or an image on the back cover overlaps the bar code.

Quality Check

Any issues with your cover or file interior will be listed here.

Note. In the top right corner, you have the option to **Download a Print PDF Proof**.

I would strongly recommend that you do this so that you can preview the file on your computer and check the details, as well as online within the KDP system.

Go through each page of the online proof and make sure that you are happy with how your print book appears and that it matches perfectly with the print-ready PDF that you uploaded onto the KDP system.

For example, check that the dropped cap at the beginning of the first paragraph of a new chapter has been carried over and the paragraph indent is in place.

If you have images in your novel, the system will reject your manuscript if the quality is not at least 300dpi.

What if you need to change something in your print book?

The only way to change the paperback proof for your book is to go back to the original text document, make the change, save the document, save it as a new PDF and then load the PFD file onto the KDP Paperback manuscript page.

Then repeat the Book Preview process and check that the paperback now meets all the quality standards and is how you want it to appear.

When you are happy with the online proof, click Approve.

At this point you will also see a **Summary** of the book details that you have entered and the basic printing costs for one copy in your Amazon marketplace.

This is very useful because it instantly gives you an idea of how much you should charge for your paperback. The detailed royalty payments are listed on the next page.

For example.

You can then save the Book Content page and click **Save and Continue** onto Paperback Book Rights, Pricing and Distribution. Then **SAVE AS DRAFT.**

Setting a Price for Your Paperback Novel

This should be both a strategic and a market-based decision.

It is always worth taking the time to review the latest Amazon.com bestseller list for similar books in your particular fiction or non-fiction niche and make a note of the price range for print books of similar page count.

In most cases it is best to use the Amazon.com marketplace as the primary market for your novel and then base the price in the other markets based on the US dollar price you want to charge.

If you click on the chevron next to the "**6 other marketplaces**" you will be given an estimate of the royalty payment you can expect from sales in each market. Now is the time to adjust the pricing in a particular market if you wish to move away from the default price based on the dollar conversion. For example, the UK currently imposes 20% VAT on digital downloads such as eBooks but print books are not subject to tax. Other countries may have different rules.

The current list at the time of writing includes the Amazon stores in USA, UK, Germany, France, Italy, Spain and Japan.

Pricing & Royalty						
	Primary Marketplace	List Price		Rate	Printing	Royalty
	Amazon.com ⇅	$ 7.99 USD		60%	$2.21	$2.59
		Min. $3.68, Max. $250.00 ▾ Base all marketplaces on this price				
	Expanded Distribution ▾	☐		40%	$2.21	$0.99

Expanded Distribution.

By clicking the Expanded Distribution box on this page, you will enable Expanded Distribution for your paperback through bookstores, online retailers, libraries, and academic institutions.

The royalty rate is 40% of the book's list price effective in the distribution channel at the time of purchase, minus printing costs, applicable taxes, and withholding charges.

There is, of course, no guarantee that your novel will be ordered outside of Amazon since Amazon does not market or promote your work in other outlets or stores.

Eligibility. As mentioned earlier, you will need to have registered yourself as a publisher and purchased your own ISBN numbers in order to use the Expanded Distribution system.

The trim size of your book must also meet the specified list of dimensions.

Note: If you enable Expanded Distribution, it can take up to six to eight weeks for your book to become available through the Expanded Distribution channels.

You can find out more here on the KDP page for this topic:

https://kdp.amazon.com/en_US/help/topic/GQTT4W3T5AYK7L45

It is strongly recommended that you order a printed author proof copy of your novel before you proceed with the final approval.

Depending on your location your proof can take one or two weeks to arrive, but it worth waiting to see what your book will look like to a reader who has bought a copy from the online store.

One of the advantages of using Amazon Print is that they have local printers close to your home store which cuts down the print time compared to CreateSpace where printed proofs could take 3 weeks to arrive in the UK or other international locations from the USA.

I know that a week or two sounds like a long time when you are anxious to get your novel published as a paperback print book, but it is always time well spent.

It is *amazing* how many typos or tiny formatting errors leap out when you have the printed book in your hand. If possible, ask someone else to read the book and point out any errors or points where clarification is needed. It is much better that you find them, rather than a reader. The reading experience to your customer should be as good as the experience that they expect from a traditional publisher.

This is the advantage of self-publishing your own print books. You can quickly edit your manuscript, save it as a PDF and upload it to KDP Print without having to wait for someone else to do that work for you.

Go through the online proof process one more time, then approve your proof paperback and proceed to the next stage of paperback rights, pricing and distribution.

Last Step. Click on Publish Your Paperback Book.

The book will then enter the Review phase where it will be checked before final approval from Amazon KDP Print. Be aware, even if your online proof looks fine, the review team may find an error on the cover or interior which means that they cannot approve your paperback until you have corrected the fault. Cover faults tend to be when the text goes into the bleed area. Fonts should always be embedded when you create the PDF file of your text.

They will email you with full details of any changes that need to be made and when your book is full approved.

Paperback Details	Paperback Content	Paperback Rights & Pricing
✓ Complete	✓ Complete	✓ Complete

Territories

Select the territories for which you hold distribution rights. Learn more about distribution rights.

⦿ **All territories (worldwide rights)** What are worldwide rights? ▾

◯ Individual territories What are Individual Territory rights? ▾

Pricing & Royalty

Primary Marketplace	List Price		Rate	Printing	Royalty
Amazon.com ⇅	$ 7.99	USD	60%	$3.48	$1.32
	Min. $5.80, Max. $250.00 ▾ Base all marketplaces on this price				
Expanded Distribution ▾	☐		40%	$3.48	n/a
6 other marketplaces					⌄

Terms & Conditions

It can take up to 72 hours for your book to be available for purchase on Amazon. Until then, the book's status will be "In Review" on your Bookshelf.

By clicking publish I confirm that I agree to and am in compliance with the KDP Terms and Conditions.

✓ **Proof Copies: Click here to request a proof copy** of this book, which you can purchase through your Amazon cart. Learn more

< Back to Content	Save as Draft	Publish Your Paperback Book

Congratulations! You have now formatted and published your own paperback book!

SUMMARY AND CONCLUSIONS FOR KDP PRINT

I hope that I have demonstrated in this short section how the KDP print on demand platform offers an easy way for authors to produce beautiful looking paperbacks with professional styling. And you can be certain that your file will be accepted by KDP when you are ready to publish your novel.

Yes, you still need to strip out all the original formatting you used when you wrote the text before you start, but this is an essential step. Then use the formatting tools described in this book to design the interior and exterior of your paperback so that your readers will be delighted with their purchase.

Create a new copy of your manuscript and take an hour to play with the system and find out if Kindle publishing works for you and your specific project.

The best thing to do is experiment and have fun! You can change the trim size and cover design as many times as you like, but you will need to create a new PDF cover flat for each test. And don't forget to order a proof copy before you click on the *Publish Your Paperback Book* Button.

Any questions? The KDP support team respond very quickly to any questions you may have, no matter how simple. It is their business to support indie authors and get them into print and online as quickly as possible.

Happy publishing!

PART THREE. HOW TO USE THE KINDLE CREATE TOOL TO FORMAT AND PUBLISH EBOOKS AND PRINT BOOKS

26

INTRODUCTION TO KINDLE CREATE

Discover the fast way to format your Word manuscript into both a Kindle eBook and Paperback print book using the free Kindle Create Software provided by Amazon Kindle Direct Publishing (KDP).

Kindle Create takes indie publishing on the Amazon platform to the next level. Your manuscript will be transformed into both a professional looking eBook and a paperback book using custom themes with chapter titles, drop caps and image placement options.

Why Kindle Create?

Kindle Create transforms your text document into a file format which is acceptable for both the Kindle eBook of your novel and the paperback print on demand format of your novel or novella.

You don't need to learn about coding or how to calculate margins or special formatting to design the interior of the paperback print version of your work, the software tool takes care of all of that automatically for you.

It has been designed by Amazon specifically to support indie authors and to help them publish their work quickly and easily.

In this section you will find step by step instructions on how to use Kindle Create to:

• Publish both your eBook and paperback using the Amazon Kindle Direct Publishing (KDP) platform and Kindle Create.

• Format your text with styles and themes.

• Automatically create a clickable table of contents for your eBook.

• Automatically create a page number table of contents for your paperback print book.

• Add or edit text.

• Add, delete, resize, and/or align images.

• Preview how your eBook will display on tablets, phones, and Kindle E-readers and create a file to publish to KDP.

By using the Amazon custom software, you can be confident that your work will meet all of Amazon's requirements.

Throughout this section, I will use a real case study of my own mystery novel to demonstrate how Kindle Create works in practice.

How to Download the Kindle Create tool.

You can find the instructions on how to download the conversion tool in two places:

On the Kindle Direct Publishing (KDP) Website. https://kdp.amazon.com

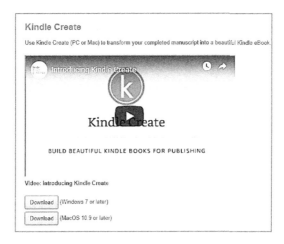

From inside the Amazon.com Kindle store. https://amzn.to/2t44YRg

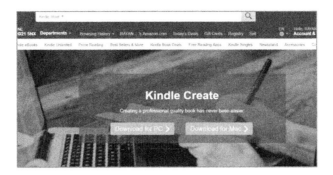

Windows

Click the **Download Now** button. A confirmation box appears. Click **Save File**.

You will be prompted to save the installer to your **Downloads** folder, but you can change the location. Click **Save**.

Open your **Downloads** folder (or the location you saved the installer to) and double-click the installer file.

The installation wizard opens. Read through the License Agreement and click **I Agree** if you accept the terms.

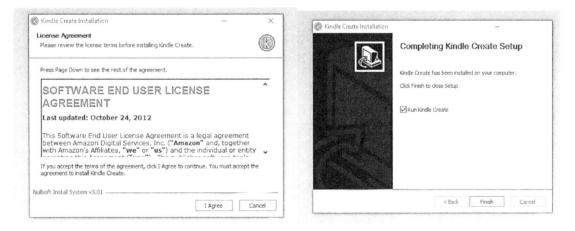

You will be prompted to install Kindle Create in a default location, but you can change the location. Click **Install**. You will receive a success message when installation is complete.

The **Run Kindle Create** box is checked by default, but you can change this. Click **Finish**.

MacOS

Click the **Download Now** button. Download begins. Click the **Show Downloads** button.

Double-click the installer file. The installation wizard opens.

Click **Continue**.

Read through the License Agreement, click **Continue**, and then click **Agree** if you accept the terms.

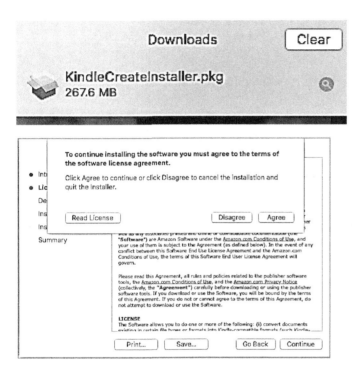

You will be prompted to install Kindle Create in a default location, but you can change the location. Click **Continue** and then click **Install**.

You will receive a success message when installation is complete. Click **Close**

After installation, you can launch Kindle Create by selecting **Windows key > Amazon > Kindle Create** (Windows) or **Launchpad > Kindle Create** (Mac).

27

GETTING STARTED ON KINDLE CREATE

To create a new project from a .doc(x) file.

On the Kindle Create launch screen, click the **New Project from File** button.

You can also launch a new project by selecting **File > New Project** or using the shortcut CTRL + N (CMD + N for Mac users).

In the **Content Language** list, select the language of your book. (This does not change the language of the Kindle Create menus.)

The Choose File dialog box is displayed. Select the Novels, Essays, Poetry, Narrative Non-Fiction option.

Click the **Choose File** button, navigate to the .doc(x) file of your novel on your computer system, select the file, and click **Open**.

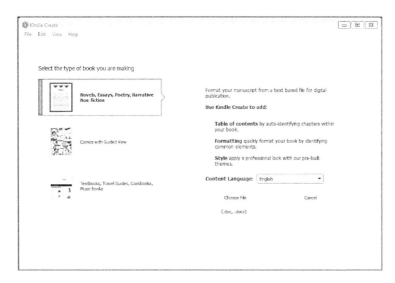

Once you have selected a file, Kindle Create begins converting it to a Kindle eBook.

The conversion system optimizes font faces, line spacing, margins, indents, and other typography features to improve reading on electronic devices. It also converts every page break that you have inserted in your .doc(x) file into a new section.

While your file is being imported, Kindle Create displays rotating screens that tell you more about Kindle Create. When conversion finishes, the **Import Successful** dialog box is displayed.

Click the Continue button.

Automatic Chapter Recognition and the Table of Contents

Click the **Get Started** button and Kindle Create begins finding potential **Chapter Title** elements in your eBook.

The **Automatic Chapter Titles** dialog box is displayed.

The conversion system reads the header 1 style as a chapter title.

This is your chance to check that the list of chapter titles is correct – this is important since it will be used to automatically create the table of contents for your book.

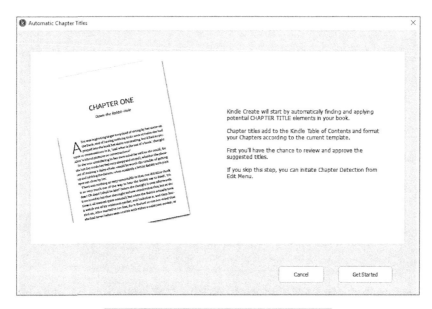

Automatic Chapter Titles

Kindle Create will start by automatically finding and applying potential CHAPTER TITLE elements in your book.

Chapter titles add to the Kindle Table of Contents and format your Chapters according to the current template.

First you'll have the chance to review and approve the suggested titles.

If you skip this step, you can initiate Chapter Detection from Edit Menu.

Cancel   Get Started

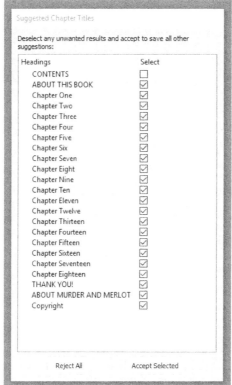

Suggested Chapter Titles

Deselect any unwanted results and accept to save all other suggestions:

Headings	Select
CONTENTS	☐
ABOUT THIS BOOK	☑
Chapter One	☑
Chapter Two	☑
Chapter Three	☑
Chapter Four	☑
Chapter Five	☑
Chapter Six	☑
Chapter Seven	☑
Chapter Eight	☑
Chapter Nine	☑
Chapter Ten	☑
Chapter Eleven	☑
Chapter Twelve	☑
Chapter Thirteen	☑
Chapter Fourteen	☑
Chapter Fifteen	☑
Chapter Sixteen	☑
Chapter Seventeen	☑
Chapter Eighteen	☑
THANK YOU!	☑
ABOUT MURDER AND MERLOT	☑
Copyright	☑

Reject All   Accept Selected

The **Suggested Chapter Titles** dialog box displays a list of possible chapter titles.

Uncheck any items that are not chapter headings and then click **Accept Selected**.

The checked items will be part of the Kindle Interactive table of contents.

For example. In the case study novel, I did not want the CONTENTS page to be included in the Table of Contents, so I unchecked that box.

From this dialog box, you can also click a chapter heading to go to that section and apply formatting while keeping the **Suggested Chapter Titles** dialog box open.

You can now go through the help tutorials or dive in.

28

SELECT A KINDLE CREATE THEME

Next to the Save button in the top right header bar is the **THEME button.**

The Modern theme is the default active theme, but you can use one of the other three themes if you prefer: Classic, Amour and Cosmos.

For most novels, Modern or Amour works well, but you should take the time to experiment and select each theme in turn. If you don't like how that theme looks, use the UNDO arrow at the top left of the page to return to the Modern theme.

Language note: If your .doc(x) file is in one of the supported Indic languages (Hindi, Tamil, Malayalam, Marathi, or Gujarati), Kindle Create only displays **Classic** and **Modern**.

The Default Modern Theme

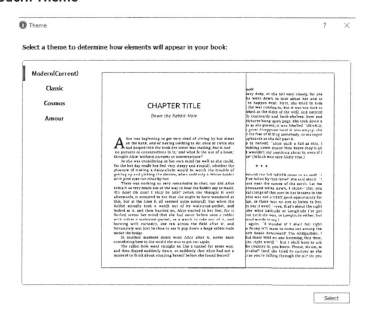

There are four aspects of each theme that you should look out for:

• **The Chapter Title.** Always in uppercase but compare the font used. Does this font match with the genre of your novel?

• **The Chapter Subtitle.** Lower case or uppercase? Italics or straight?

• **The body text styling.** The standard Kindle body text style is fully justified. You can add a paragraph indent to break up the large blocks of text.

• **The scene separator** style.

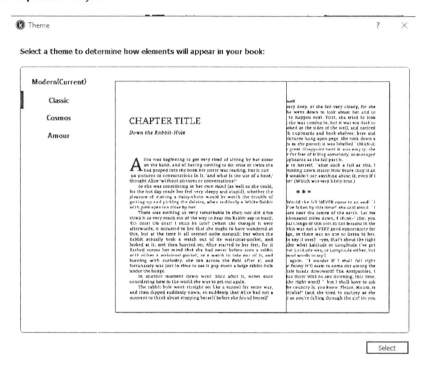

For example. In **the Classic Theme** you will notice that both the chapter title and the subheading use a serif font, are left aligned and the subheading is in italics.

This is in contrast to the Modern theme where the chapter title is centred and uses a non-serif font. The scene separator is made up of 3 large centred asterisks.

Compare these themes **the Amour theme.** The chapter title is a very decorative Grand Vibes font and centred. The subtitle is also serif and centred. The scene separator symbol uses the decorative Grand Vibes font.

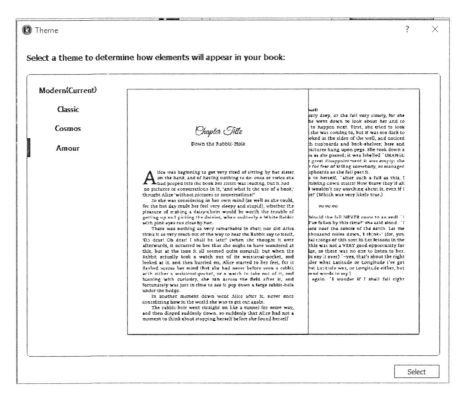

On the other hand, you may be writing science fiction or fantasy and prefer a non-serif font and more graphic approach in **The Cosmos Theme.** The choice is entirely yours.

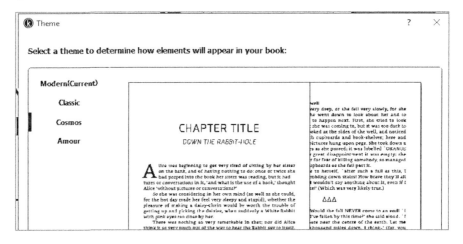

29

FORMATTING AND CUSTOMISING THE FRONT MATTER USING KINDLE CREATE

The simplest way to format your eBook is to start at the beginning of the book and work through the book one section at a time.

You can easily change the appearance of every element in the book and the theme that you have selected using the Formatting options on the right-hand side panel.

Components of a published book: The front matter, the body text and the back matter.

The Front Matter
This is also called the **Preliminary Matter**. Basically, the front matter is everything that precedes the main text of your book. The front matter in a modern eBook is usually very short and simple.

In Kindle Create, the front matter pages are called Book Start Elements and there are pre-formatted styles for several of the following elements.

<u>Formatting the Front Matter</u>
The Title Page. This has the title of your book, a subtitle, if you are using one, and the name of the author. You can also insert an author or publisher brand image on the title page.

The Copyright Page.
Please refer to chapter three of this book for full details on the Copyright page and ISBN numbers.

Praise for the book from leading authors in your niche. (Optional. These reviews will be listed as editorial reviews on the book description page.)

Dedication. This is the personal dedication written by the author. (Optional)

About the book. This is written by the author and should set out the scope and objectives of the book. (Optional)

Note from the Author. Optional but very useful for indie authors who use this page to introduce their book and/or offer a free reader magnet if the reader subscribes to your mailing list.

The intention is to invite readers from Amazon to click over to your website or an opt-in page which you control. If you have this invitation early in the book, it will be included in the "Look Inside" sample. Note. This is also repeated in the back matter at the end of the book.

Acknowledgements. Most fiction authors move this to the back of the eBook.

Table of Contents.
The wording of each entry should match the headings in the text of the book.

The electronic table of contents will be generated automatically by Kindle Create so you do not have to create one in the text of your document.

Lists of illustrations, figures and maps. Especially useful for children's books and fantasy novels.

Epigraph Quotation
An epigraph is a relevant quotation which is added to the start of the book, or each chapter or part of the book. It is formatted differently from the rest of the text so that it stands out.

Front Matter Examples

Worked Examples from Case Study eBook. A Short Mystery Novel

You will note that this is the first book in a new cozy mystery series and I wanted the readers to recognise that the second book was already written and available. Readers love series and prefer to invest their time in a book where others in the series are available. There is an exclusive sample of the beginning of book two at the end of this book. I also offer free review copies and bonus content to my mailing list subscribers.

MURDER AND MOZZARELLA

SOPHIE BRENT

COZY MYSTERY AUTHOR

ABOUT THIS BOOK

The 1st book in the NEW Kingsmede Cozy Murder Mystery series!

What do you do when your elderly Italian godmother is accused of murdering the chef brought in to replace her - and she probably did it?

This book will delight fans of TV shows like 'Midsomer Murders' and 'Murder She Wrote' who love reading cozy mysteries such as the Agatha Raisin and Peridale Café series.

Lottie Brannigan thought that life was complicated enough when all she had to cope with were her friends and the latest antics of her Italian relatives, but then she finds her neighbor knocked out on his doorstep and her godmother is accused of murdering a rival chef!
Running an Italian deli in an English country village has never been so deadly!
***

WOULD YOU LIKE *FREE* COPIES OF FUTURE BOOKS BY SOPHIE BRENT, EXCLUSIVE NEWS AND GIVEAWAYS? Pop along to my website and join my Reader Group! SophieBrent.com

Formatting the Front Matter with Kindle Create

Formatting the Title Page

This was how the title page looked when I uploaded the case study novel.

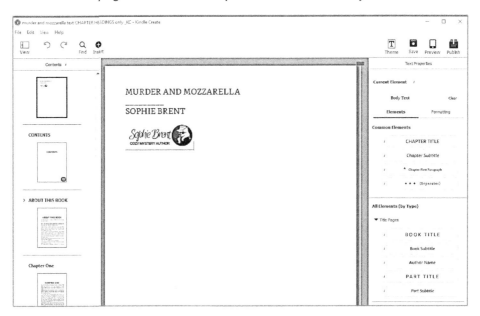

When I applied the Amour Theme it was converted into this page. To me, the title is too decorative and hard to read. Time to use the formatting tool to change the font.

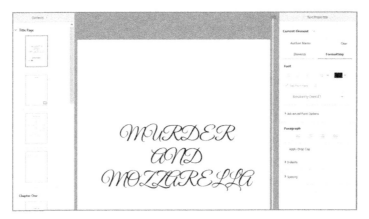

Customise the Book Title Page

In the Text Properties Sidebar on the right you will see a list of **Elements** for the **Title Pages.**

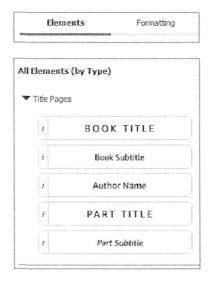

These Elements are pre-formatted template pages which you can use to format each part of your novel.

There are five options for the Title Pages.

Highlight your book title and click on *Book Title*. Then *Formatting* to customise the book title for your genre.

Within the Amour theme, you can Change Grand Vibes to one of three other options: - Bookerly (serif). Amazon Ember (sans serif) and Monospace. You will recall that the text of an eBook has to be reflowable so that it can be customised by the reader. So, Amazon does not provide a lot of choice here.

Save the document after each element has been formatted.

Example using the Bookerly font which was the one I went for. Simple and clean and serif to match the serif book text font.

Formatting the Subtitle of your book

If you have a subtitle, you can format it using the same process as the main title.

Highlight the sub-title text.

Go to the right-hand side bar and *Elements*. Select the *Subtitle element*.

Kindle Create will add custom formatting for the subtitle and position it in the correct place relative to the title and the title page.

Not happy with how it looks in this theme? Then select *Formatting* in the header bar if you want to customise the subtitle font.

Formatting your Author Name

Follow the same process as for the main title and subtitle.

Highlight/ select the author name.

Go to the right-hand side bar and *Elements*.

Select the *Author Name* element.

Kindle Create will add custom formatting for the name and position it in the correct place relative to the book title and the title page.

Then you can use the *Formatting* option if you want to customise the font.

Be sure to save your document after working on each element.

Formatting the About the Book Page

The Amour theme created a very decorative header for this page which I thought would be difficult to read, especially as a digital file on a mobile phone, so I replaced it with another Front Matter element. *Page Title Template.*

The alternative was to use the Formatting tool and selecting another font.

Formatting the Note from the Author and Other Optional Pages

Use the same technique for the About Page and customise the font and layout until you are happy with the appearance.

The Heading of the page will appear in the Table of Contents if you select it as a chapter heading.

30

ADDING AND EDITING IMAGES USING KINDLE CREATE

The Kindle Create tool is ideal for text-heavy documents such as novels and many non-fiction books, but it does allow you to insert, resize and delete images in your book.

Many authors include their professional author photo on the About the Author page in their book or use images as illustrations. For example. On the title page in the case study, I included an image of my brand logo below the author name.

The best place for an image is inserted below a block of text as a stand-alone image "in line" with the text.

The images should be:

• Jpeg format (jpg)

• at least 100 pixels long but usually larger

• ideally 300ppi to make sure that they do not appear blurry on the newer higher resolution Kindle devices

• not wrapped around or inside text.

To add a JPG image to your eBook
Right-click the location where you want to insert the JPG image and select *Insert Image* from the pop-up menu.

The Insert Image window appears. Choose the image you want to add and click *Open*. The Image Properties are then displayed in the Properties Pane.

Image Properties
<u>**Alternative Text.**</u> This is a few lines of text to help blind or visually impaired users to know what the image is about and why it is in this book. If the image is purely decorative, such as a flourish under the title of the book or chapter headings, or a decorative page border, you can check the box to exclude it from the screen reader.

<u>**Image Size.**</u> Select one of the display size options for your image. There are multiple options ranging from Small (33%) to Full (100%).

<u>**Image Position**</u>. In the case study eBook, I want the Medium sized image to be placed in the centre of the page under the author name. Large and Full images are automatically centred.

If you want this to be a full width image, click on the Full option. Additional options will then appear in the Image Properties menu.

Bleed for eBooks.

Bleed images are images which extend beyond the pre-set margins of your page to the outside of the paper in print books.

Using bleed on full-page images in a .doc(x) file is currently a pre-release beta feature within Kindle Create.

Place within Margin. This is the normal default and will ensure that your image is central on the page and within the margins and viewing experience for your reader on whatever Kindle device or app they are using.

Place to Edge. Placing to edge will lock the content into the portrait orientation for this book which means that customers can only read your book in portrait mode. Amazon is working on this issue, but you need to be aware of it.

To replace an image, right-click the image and select *Replace Image* from the pop-up menu.

Go to *Edit* in left header menu.

Click on the *Insert +* button. Then *insert Image from file*.

To delete an image, right-click the image and select *Delete Image* from the pop-up menu.

31

FORMATTING THE BODY TEXT INSIDE KINDLE CREATE

The Body of the eBook

Each new chapter should have a chapter title and will start on a new page. Then the body text of your novel follows within each chapter.

If you have a very long book, then you can use Parts to divide sections of the book and start each part on a new page.

The Kindle Create tool provides two standard serif and two non-serif fonts for the header style and the body text.

The serif fonts are Bookerly or Grand Vibes for the header font and Bookerly for the body text. The non-serif fonts are Amazon Ember and Monospace.

It will then be up to the reader to select the font they prefer from the range offered by their Amazon Kindle reader or app. Kindle Create provides six templates you can use to format the text of your book.

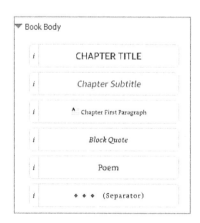

Formatting the Chapter Headings
Chapter Heading Styling

I selected the **Amour theme** for this book, which is a contemporary cozy mystery novel, so I decided to use this styling which uses the Grand Vibes font for the chapter headings.

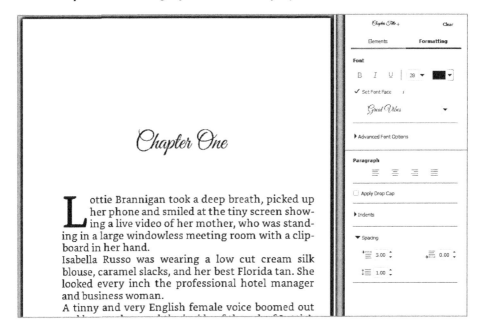

First Paragraph Styling
To insert a drop cap to the first letter in a new chapter.

Select the first paragraph of the text of your novel, then click on Elements to go back to the main menu.

Then click on *Chapter First Paragraph* in *Book Body* options.

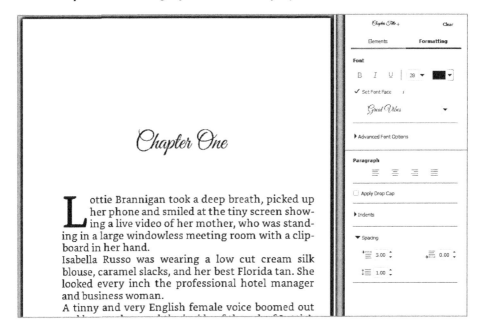

The drop cap for the first letter seems to be too large to me. I have reduced it to 2 rows which I prefer. In the second box to the right, you can set the space between the drop cap letter and the rest of the word.

I prefer it to be close for fiction, but this is a personal choice and some authors may select a very large drop cap and gap.

As with all these controls, try changing the settings and see how the text looks. You can always go back and undo the change.

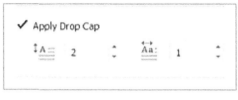

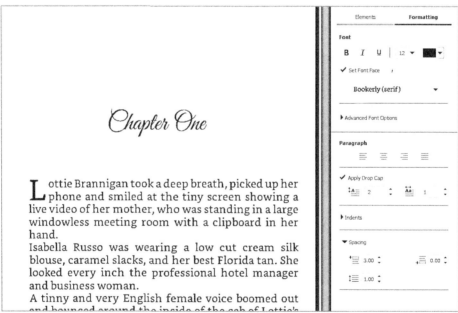

Save your document.

Now go to every chapter and repeat the process so that the drop cap is set-up the same way in the first paragraph of every new chapter in your book.

If you do this now, you won't forget. Consistency if very important – every chapter should look the same to create a great digital reading experience for your reader.

Save your document frequently.

Formatting the Body Text

If you formatted your document as described in the previous section when we created a very clean version of your text, then this stage should already be complete.

Your novel can look different, however, when it is loaded onto Kindle Create.

So, this is your opportunity to make final adjustments on how you want the text to appear in your Kindle eBook. It is a laborious process since you have to go through every chapter and make the updates.

Worked Example.

Highlight a paragraph.

The Font is Bookerly (serif) for this text which works well for a novel.

Size. You can reduce the size of the font or increase it.

Paragraph Indent. Experiment with the options until you have the appearance you are looking for. For example.

> L ottie Brannigan took a deep breath, picked up her phone and smiled at the tiny screen showing a live video of her mother, who was standing in a large windowless meeting room with a clipboard in her hand.
>
> Isabella Russo was wearing a low cut cream silk blouse, caramel slacks, and her best Florida tan. She looked every inch the professional hotel manager and business woman.

In this paragraph I have reduced the font to 11 point from 12 point which was the default for this theme and added a first line indent of 3 point. But kept the text fully justified.

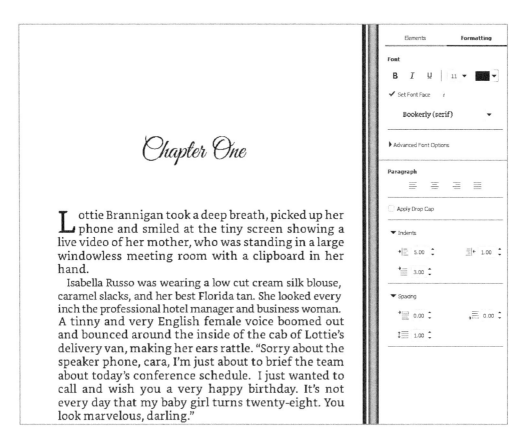

To apply this to the entire chapter, highlight all the body text in the chapter and make the change. Then repeat the process for the body text in every other chapter in the same way.

Take care not to select the chapter heading or these will also be changed.

Line Spacing. To add space between the paragraphs use this setting:

Large blocks of text are much easier to read if there is a small gap between the paragraphs.

Use the up and down arrows to increase or decrease the space between the paragraphs. For example:

L ottie Brannigan took a deep breath, picked up her
phone and smiled at the tiny screen showing a
live video of her mother, who was standing in a large
windowless meeting room with a clipboard in her
hand.

Isabella Russo was wearing a low cut cream silk
blouse, caramel slacks, and her best Florida tan. She
looked every inch the professional hotel manager
and business woman.

A tinny and very English female voice boomed out
and bounced around the inside of the cab of Lottie's
delivery van, making her ears rattle. "Sorry about the
speaker phone, cara, I'm just about to brief the team
about today's conference schedule. I just wanted to
call and wish you a very happy birthday. It's not
every day that my baby girl turns twenty-eight. You
look marvelous, darling."

Then her mother's voice faded away and her fin-

Line Spacing. To adjust line spacing between the rows of text use this setting

$$\updownarrow\equiv \quad 1.00 \quad \updownarrow$$

Adding Line Spacing between rows creates more white space on the page and can make the text easier to read. In the worked example, the text is set to single spacing which is the recommended setting that Amazon KDP prefers, but you can change it by using the Kindle Create formatting options.

For example: 1.25 lines and 1.5 line spacing.

To apply this to the entire chapter, highlight all of the body text in the chapter and make the change. Then repeat the process for the body text in every other chapter in the same way.

Yes, this is time consuming, but it is worth it to maintain a consistent style to your body text and make the electronic document easier to read.

End users can also change the line spacing, since this is part of the customisation options offered to readers on Kindle readers and Kindle apps on various devices.

windowless meeting room with a clipboard in her hand.

Isabella Russo was wearing a low cut cream silk blouse, caramel slacks, and her best Florida tan. She looked every inch the professional hotel manager and business woman.

A tinny and very English female voice boomed out and bounced around the inside of the cab of Lottie's delivery van, making her ears rattle. "Sorry about the speaker phone, cara, I'm just about to brief the team about today's conference schedule. I just wanted to call and wish you a very happy birthday. It's not every day that my baby girl turns twenty-eight. You

hand.

Isabella Russo was wearing a low cut cream silk blouse, caramel slacks, and her best Florida tan. She looked every inch the professional hotel manager and business woman.

A tinny and very English female voice boomed out and bounced around the inside of the cab of Lottie's delivery van, making her ears rattle. "Sorry about the speaker phone, cara, I'm just about to brief the team about today's conference schedule. I just wanted to

The Scene Separator Symbol

Many eBook authors use 3 asterisks *** or other text symbols to indicate when a scene ends within a chapter.

Kindle Create provides decorative separators to indicate a transition in the text.

The style of the separator varies according to the theme that you have selected. Each theme has a different scene separator symbol which has been designed to match the styling of the chapter headings and font.

Classic Theme Separator

He paused. "The police will be back in about an hour and want us to make a list of anything that could be missing. If it's okay with you I'd like to get that done as quickly as possible, although I should warn you, the place is a mess. If you are up to it, would you mind coming in and taking a look?"

* * *

The word mess didn't prepare Lottie for the total chaos that hit her when she walked into Lucien's living room.

The apartment had been completely turned over. Every drawer in every room, every bookshelf, and every cupboard had been opened and the contents flung out.

For Amour – the style I am using for this novel, the separator is:

He paused. "The police will be back in about an hour and want us to make a list of anything that could be missing. If it's okay with you I'd like to get that done as quickly as possible, although I should warn you, the place is a mess. If you are up to it, would you mind coming in and taking a look?"

The word mess didn't prepare Lottie for the total chaos that hit her when she walked into Lucien's living room.

The apartment had been completely turned over. Every drawer in every room, every bookshelf, and every cupboard had been opened and the contents flung out.

Modern Theme Separator

He paused. "The police will be back in about an hour and want us to make a list of anything that could be missing. If it's okay with you I'd like to get that done as quickly as possible, although I should warn you, the place is a mess. If you are up to it, would you mind coming in and taking a look?"

◆ ◆ ◆

The word mess didn't prepare Lottie for the total chaos that hit her when she walked into Lucien's living room.

The apartment had been completely turned over. Every drawer in every room, every bookshelf, and every cupboard had been opened and the contents flung out.

Cosmos Theme Separator

He paused. "The police will be back in about an hour and want us to make a list of anything that could be missing. If it's okay with you I'd like to get that done as quickly as possible, although I should warn you, the place is a mess. If you are up to it, would you mind coming in and taking a look?"

ΔΔΔ

The word mess didn't prepare Lottie for the total chaos that hit her when she walked into Lucien's living room.

The apartment had been completely turned over. Every drawer in every room, every bookshelf, and every cupboard had been opened and the contents flung out.

Note – you cannot format the separator. It is built into the theme design.

32

FORMATTING THE BACK MATTER OF YOUR BOOK USING KINDLE CREATE

The Back Matter for eBooks
The back matter of an indie eBook will typically follow this sequence:

Any acknowledgements. (Optional)

A list of other books from the author.

Note from the author, thanking the reader for buying the book and asking them to leave a review on the online store where they bought the book.

Offer a free reader magnet if the reader subscribes to your mailing list.

About the Author page with links to your website and social media profile pages, where there will be more opportunities to take the reader away from Amazon and onto your mailing list. You can add an author photo here if you wish.

Just as the Front Matter was called the Book Start Elements, the **Back Matter is called the Book End Pages in the Elements Options.**

Click on Elements to go back to the main menu.

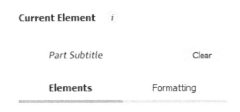

Back Matter Examples

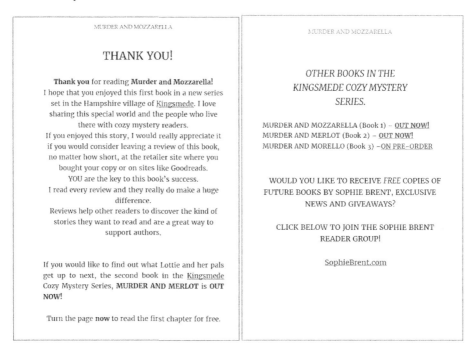

If you marked the title of each page in the back matter as Heading 1 in your manuscript before you uploaded it into Kindle Create, this formatting should carry across as the

Chapter or Page Title. If you want to change the font or font size, click on the *Formatting* option.

In this example of a Thank You page, I used a Page Title template which has a sans serif font, Amazon Ember, to make the heading stand out. You will also note that I did not use any paragraph indentation since this is not body text.

I did add a small space between the paragraphs to break up the text.

You could apply the same customisation to any of your back-matter pages.

Great! Now it's time to Preview what your novel will look like as a Kindle eBook.

33

USE KINDLE PREVIEWER TO PREVIEW YOUR FORMATTED KINDLE EBOOK

You can preview what your Kindle eBook will look like to a reader at any time by clicking the Preview button in the right header bar. You will be taken the Kindle Previewer Inspector screen. For example.

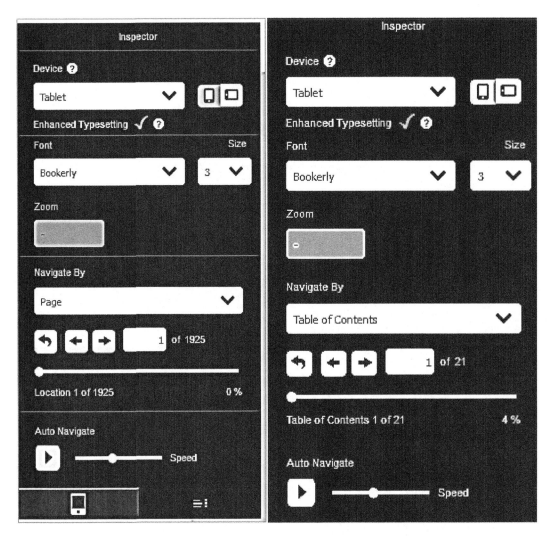

As you can see there is a wide range of preview options to select from.

I usually check that <u>the tablet and the phone preview</u> for the opening pages and the first chapter look okay to a reader using Bookerly font size 3 in portrait mode. To make it easier for you to read, you can increase the font size by using the arrow on the size button.

Important. Be Sure to Check that the Table of Contents page is correct.

Kindle Create will automatically generate an electronic clickable table of contents for your novel based on the Heading 1 styles you set in your manuscript and when you uploaded your file.

Go to the *Navigate By* option and click the chevron and then *Table of Contents*.

This is how your reader will go through your novel so if any you need to go back to your file and change the page or chapter headings or delete entries in the Table of Contents, now is the time to do it.

Work through the eBook and make any changes to your text or layout then Preview the eBook again. Once you are happy with the book preview, save your file. You can move on to the final step.

34

EXPORT YOUR KINDLE EBOOK TO KDP FOR PUBLISHING AS A KINDLE EBOOK.

Click on *the Publish* Button in the top header menu bar.

Kindle Create will save a "package" of your formatted book as a KPF file to your desktop or your specified location. Look out for **the. kpf extension** on your document.

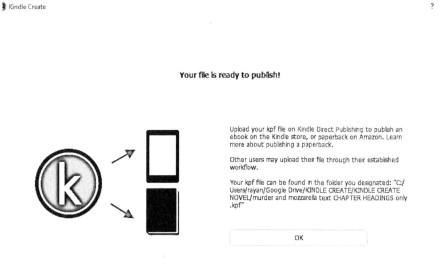

To publish your eBook using Kindle Direct Publishing, follow the instructions given in chapter four of this book, but when you come to the Book Content page, **upload the .kpf Kindle Create file you have just created for your manuscript instead of a Word .doc(x) file.**

All of the other instructions remain the same.

35

BUILDING THE KDP PRINT PAPERBACK BOOK USING A BETA VERSION OF THE STANDARD KINDLE CREATE TOOL

One of the advantages of the Kindle Create tool is that you can publish both an eBook and a paperback format of your book with the same manuscript file.

Kindle Create also takes care of complicated paperback formatting tasks for you and you can publish it in any trim size offered by Amazon KDP Print.

When you upload your Kindle Create (.kpf) file to KDP, margins are automatically calculated, and page numbers are added to your paperback's table of contents page and footers. Your first chapter will start on a right-facing page, with subsequent chapters starting on the next available page. You can also use the KDP Previewer tool to review the online proof of your print book.

Because this option is still being developed by Amazon it is only accessible if you turn on the Early Access option in the Preferences setting inside Kindle Create.

Current Limitations include:
This feature is designed for text-heavy books with a simple layout such as novels, essays and memoirs that you want to publish in both eBook and paperback format.

It is not designed to work well with paperbacks which include complex tables, footnotes, or endnotes.

• The font and font size for paperbacks can't be changed.

• You won't be able to customize the margins, headers, page numbers, and font.

• Margins will be automatically calculated to meet the KDP specifications for a print book of that trim size and number of pages. The margins cannot be changed.

• Left-page headers will show the author name, right-page headers the book title.

• The alignment and style of the author name and book title can't be changed.

• Page numbers are automatically added to the footer. They'll start on the first page of your book's first chapter.

• You should have already set-up your Kindle eBook inside KDP, following the instructions given in chapter four of this book. You do not need to publish your eBook, but all of the Book Details should have been entered for the eBook format of your book.

To use this feature, open Kindle Create and turn on Early Access:
Windows. Choose Help > Settings > Early Access

Mac. Choose Kindle Create > Preferences > Early Access, then check the Enable Beta Features box.

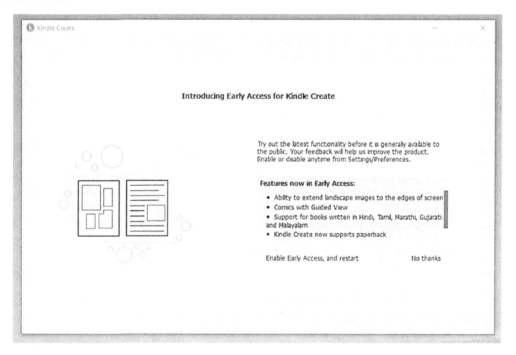

Click on **Enable Early Access and restart**.

You'll be taken back to the main Start screen.

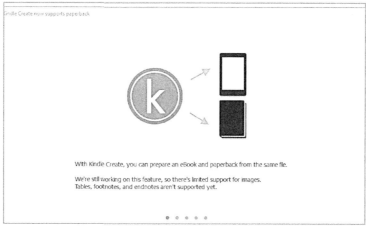

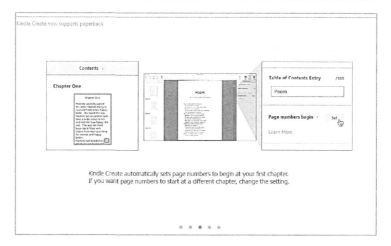

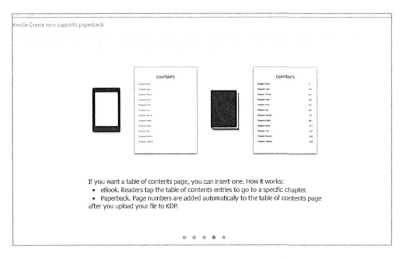

If you want a table of contents page, you can insert one. How it works:
- eBook. Readers tap the table of contents entries to go to a specific chapter.
- Paperback. Page numbers are added automatically to the table of contents page after you upload your file to KDP.

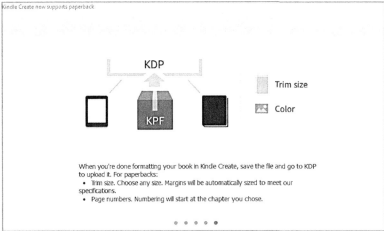

When you're done formatting your book in Kindle Create, save the file and go to KDP to upload it. For paperbacks:
- Trim size. Choose any size. Margins will be automatically sized to meet our specifications.
- Page numbers. Numbering will start at the chapter you chose.

Upload your file to KDP

Go to your Amazon KDP Bookshelf and under the Kindle eBook heading for the title of your book on the Bookshelf you will see a dotted box which says *+ Create paperback*.

Click on this box. You will be taken to the **Paperback Set-up pages.**

Paperback Details

All the information you provide for your Kindle eBook will be carried over to the paperback book details page, but you can edit the book description text and change the categories if you wish.

Paperback Content Page

Follow the instructions given in chapters twenty-four and twenty-five of this book to complete the entries for:

• The Print ISBN.

• The Publication Date. Leave this blank if you are publishing your book for the first time.

• The Print Options for your printed paperback, including the colour of the paper you prefer and the trim size you have selected for your finished book.

• The Paperback Cover finish. Do you prefer matte or glossy book covers?

The Paperback Manuscript for the Book Interior

There is one major change when you are using the Kindle Create file to generate your KDP Print paperback.

Normally you would upload a PDF of your word or text document, but in this case, you are going to **Upload the same Kindle Create .KPF file that you used for your Kindle eBook.**

It will take a few minutes for the system to process your **.kpf** file.

Paperback Book Cover
Upload the print-ready PDF of your paperback book cover.

Remember this is the full cover "flat" PDF of your entire book, including the back cover, the spine text and the front cover, together with a working margin around the entire graphic design. This is described in detail in chapter twenty-four.

It will take a few minutes for the system to process your book cover file.

For example.

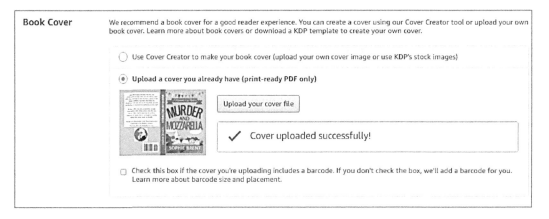

Once the book interior PDF and the book cover PDF have been loaded, the KDP system with link the two files together to create your paperback book.

Book Preview
Just as with your Kindle eBook, it is essential that you use the online Book Preview facility to check that your paperback looks the way that you want it.

Click on Launch Print Previewer.

What you will see will be a "spread" of your print book in a two-page layout, starting with the combined full book cover.

Most of the quality issues indie authors see with print on demand paperbacks are associated with the cover design rather than the content of the book.

The bar code with the ISBN will be printed in the same location every time – the bottom right corner of the book and your book will be rejected if the text on the back cover overlaps the bar code.

Quality Check

Any issues with your cover or file interior will be listed here.

Note. In the top right corner, you have the option to **download a Print PDF Proof.**

I would strongly recommend that you do this so that you can preview the file on your computer and check the details, as well as online within the KDP system.

As with your Kindle eBook, go through each page and make sure that you are happy with how your print book appears.

Kindle Create will have added automatically:

• A Table of Contents with the page numbers for each chapter/heading. By convention the table of contents will be on a right hand, odd numbered page.

• Headers with your Author Name and the Title of the book. The first page of each new chapter, by convention, does not have a header.

• Page numbers rather than electronic place indicators.

If you have used a dropped cap at the beginning of the first paragraph of a new chapter, you should check that has been carried over and the paragraph indent is in place.

For example:

CONTENTS

What if you need to change something in your print book?

The only way to change the paperback proof for your book is to go back to the original Kindle Create file, make the change, save the document, export as a new **.kpf** file and then reload the new Kindle Create KPF file onto the KDP Paperback manuscript page.

You don't need to reload the file onto the Kindle eBook system, unless you want to change the book in both formats.

Then repeat the Book Preview process and check that the paperback is how you want it.

When you are happy with the online proof, click *Approve.*
A Summary paragraph will now appear telling you the expected printing costs for your book in the trim size etc that you have specified. For example.

You can then save the Book Content page and click *Save and Continue* onto **Paperback Book Pricing and Distribution.** See chapter twenty-five for more details.

It is strongly recommended that you order a printed author proof copy of your novel before you proceed with the final approval.
Depending on your location your proof can take one or two weeks to arrive, but it worth waiting to see what your book will look like to a reader who has bought a copy from the online store.

One of the advantages of using Amazon Print is that they have local printers close to your home store which cuts down the print time compared to CreateSpace where printed proofs could take 3 weeks to arrive in the UK from the USA.
If there any changes you want to make, simply edit your Kindle Create document and reload a new file to KDP.

The reading experience to your customer should be as good as the experience that they expect from a traditional publisher.

When you are completely happy with the contents, click on the ***Publish Your Paperback Book*** button.

Your book will then be quality checked by the Amazon KDP team who will send you an email confirming the status of the review and when the book has been approved.

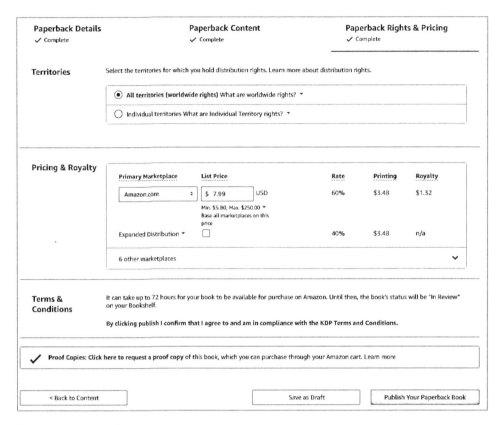

Congratulations!

You have now published your novel as both a Kindle eBook and a KDP Paperback print book.

Using Kindle Create you can customise it any way you wish to enhance the reading experience – and be certain that your book will meet KDP requirements for publishing on Amazon.

This is your book and you should be proud of it.

36

BUILDING THE KINDLE EBOOK AND THE KDP PRINT PAPERBACK OF YOUR NOVEL USING THE KINDLE CREATE ADD-IN FOR MICROSOFT WORD (PC ONLY)

For those authors who use Microsoft Word to write their novels, Kindle Create also offers a specific Add-In for Microsoft Word.

At this time of writing this guide, the Kindle Create Add-in for Microsoft Word is supported for Word 2010 and above, running on a PC only.

With Kindle Create Add-in, you can use the features inside Kindle Create that we have just explored in the stand-alone tool to format your manuscript inside of Word, without having to upload the separate Kindle Create software.

If you want to publish both an eBook and a paperback, you can upload the same .doc(x) file to KDP. The Kindle Create Add-In will automatically handle the interactive table of contents for the Kindle eBook and trim size, margins and other details for your paperback.

The tool can help you format chapter titles, first paragraph drop caps, margins, headers, and page numbers. It also lets you insert formatted pages like a copyright, dedication, and table of contents page.

Download and install Kindle Create Add-in for Microsoft Word.

To download and install the Kindle Create Add-in for Microsoft Word, visit this Amazon KDP page for more details:

https://kdp.amazon.com/en_US/help/topic/G202140110

Once the Add-in is successfully installed, you'll see that a "Kindle" tab has been added to your Word toolbar.

You can select elements of your text and apply formatting changes as we have described in the previous chapters – but without leaving Word.

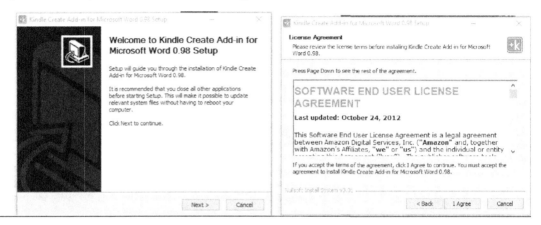

Read through the terms of the agreement, then click *I Agree* if you are happy with the contents.

Then select the folder where you want the software to be installed.

If you already have a Word document running, you will be asked to close it so that the system can install an additional menu bar to the header of your Word software.

Open the Word document for your novel.

You will notice that there is a new **Kindle** tab.in the header menu.

Click on the *Kindle tab.*

This will open a completely new menu for you with all the options that you previously saw in in the stand-alone Kindle Create tool.

Click Getting Started in the Kindle Menu.

The menu will guide you through the main steps:

Step One. Select a Theme from Classic, Modern, Amour and Cosmos as before.

Step Two. Select the Trim Options for your book. This will set up trim size, margins, font size, and indentations. Currently, there are two trim size options: 6" x 9" and 8.5" x 11".

If you want another trim size, use the recommended sizes covered in chapter thirteen and use Layout and Size Options to change the page size for the entire manuscript. Note – You cannot change the margins which are calculated by the system.

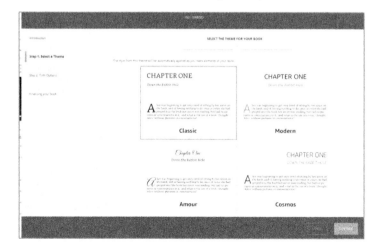

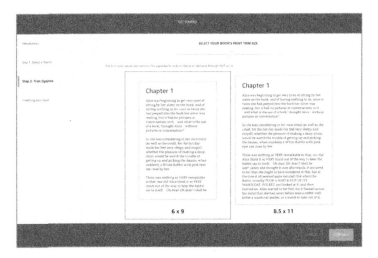

Step Three. Finalizing Your Book.

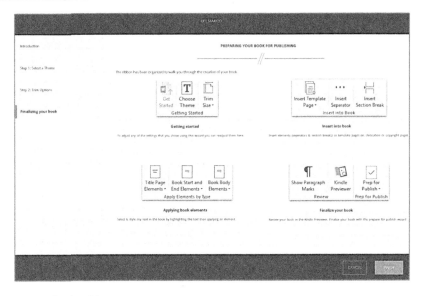

In this step you are invited to;

• Insert elements into your book, such as Template Pages, Scene Separators and Section Breaks.

• Apply and format book elements such as the Title Page, Front and Back Matter Pages and the Body Text as described in the previous chapter.

• You can then preview your eBook using the automatic Kindle Previewer from within Microsoft Word.

As soon as you hit FINISH Kindle Create will optimize your book for Kindle.

This will happen automatically and may take a few minutes.

You can then start working through your novel and using the Kindle Create menu bar to format your text

Formatting the Title Page.

Example. The book you are reading now.

Highlight the Book Title. Go to the Kindle Menu and Apply Elements by Type.

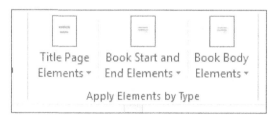

Click the **Book Title** which will be formatted according to the theme that you have selected.

Repeat this process for the Subtitle of your book if you have one, and your author name.

If you don't like the font or font size, simply select the text, go to the Home tab and then Font and change the font. For example, I preferred to use the same font that was used in the cover design to create a stronger title page for this book.

Formatting the Front and Back Matter

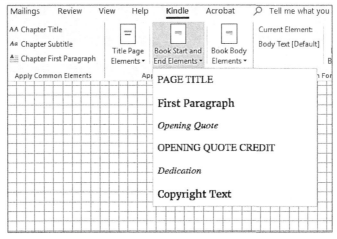

Go to the *Insert into Book* option in the Kindle menu header.

There are templates for the Dedication, Author Note and Copyright text pages.

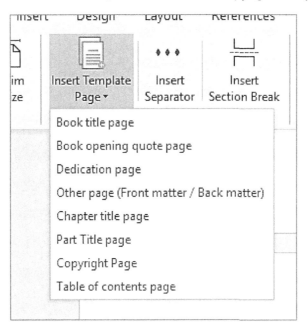

Formatting the Body of the Book

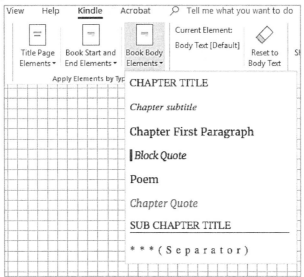

The Book Body Elements are the same as we have used before.

To Format Chapter Headings and Chapter First Paragraphs.

To apply them to your document, highlight the text or place your cursor next to the chapter heading and click *CHAPTER TITLE* in the Book Body Elements options. Your chapter heading will now be formatted according to the theme that you have chosen.

Do the same for your Subtitle if you have one.

To set a dropped cap style for the first paragraph of your chapters, highlight the text of the first paragraph or place your cursor before the first word of your first chapter and click *Chapter First Paragraph*. This will apply a drop cap to the first letter of the first word in the chapter.

Repeat these steps for each chapter in your book.

Work through your document and add formatting where needed.

To Add a Table of Contents

Select where you want to place your table of contents and click on the page that will follow your table of contents (it's usually the first chapter).

Go to the *Insert into Book* option in the Kindle menu header.

Click Insert Template Page and choose "Table of contents page."

Check that the entries are logical. If you need to add or delete entries, make any changes in the document so that the table of contents has everything you need in it and reload the table of contents page.

Add a header by clicking *Prep for Publish* option in the Kindle menu header and select Insert Headers.

 This will add your author name and book title to the tops of your pages.

Add page numbers by clicking *Prep for Publish* and select Insert Page Numbers.

This will add page numbers, beginning with your first chapter.

The Kindle Previewer

You can preview what your Kindle eBook will look like to a reader at any time by clicking the Preview button in the right header bar. You will be taken the Kindle Previewer Inspector screen which we covered in chapter ten.

When you're satisfied with your book, save your .doc(x) file. You can then upload this Word file to KDP for both your Kindle eBook and your Paperback book file.

https://kdp.amazon.com/en_US/help/topic/G202140110

Advantages of Using the free Kindle Create Add-In for Word

Kindle eBook

• **Speed.** This is the easiest and fastest way to transform your word document into a formatted file which you know that KDP will accept first time. They do all the work for you and provide the formatted pages that you need for any basic novel.

• **Preview what your Kindle eBook will look like from inside Word.** One click takes you to the Kindle Previewer which is already in your menu bar in the ribbon of your document.

• **The drop caps at the beginning of each chapter are live in the Kindle eBook**. This has traditionally been a problem with reflowable books where you can see spacing and size issues for a manually inserted drop cap on different devices.

Paperback Book

• **Fonts.** The real advantage is that, once you have assigned elements of the text, you can use the Word style sheet to change the font and font size of your entire manuscript. You are not limited to the fonts in the stand-alone Kindle Create tool.

- **Live Table of Contents.** You can see what your table of contents will look like in your printed book and immediately make edits to customise the details without leaving Word.

- **No coding or interior design skills needed.** All the interior design work is done for you automatically by Kindle Create and you don't even need to create a PDF of your Word document – the same document will upload and be accepted for both your eBook and your paperback inside KDP.

Disadvantages of Using the free Kindle Create Add-In for Word
- **System is still in Beta-Version**

This Add-In is only available for Word 2010 and newer on a Windows system pc.

- **Limited range of Paperback default trim sizes**

- **Paperback book creation**

The default settings are designed to make it as simple as possible for you to build and publish a paperback version of your book.

For most books this is not a problem. All the section breaks at the start of a new chapter have been done for you and the headers and page numbers are inserted with one click.

These defaults do mean, however, that you cannot change the interior design of your paperback such as margins and the positioning of headers and footers which will be selected according to which one of the four themes you have chosen.

Experiment! Try loading the doc. word file onto KDP and preview what your paperback looks like in the online proof. You can always change your word document and restyle it.

SUMMARY AND CONCLUSIONS ON KINDLE CREATE

I hope that I have demonstrated how Kindle Create is an easy way for authors to produce beautiful looking Kindle eBooks and paperbacks with professional styling. And you can be certain that your file will be accepted by KDP when you are ready to publish your novel.

Yes, you still need to strip out all the original formatting you used when you wrote the novel before you start, but this is an essential step to ensure that your book will read beautifully on all the Kindle devices and apps.

There are some limitations to how the Beta version of Kindle Create works for paperback formats but for most novels it is the quickest and simplest way to generate a print book – and you don't have to know anything about coding, interior print book design or how to generate a print ready PDF.

I anticipate that Amazon will improve the functionality of this option as more authors discover how Kindle Create can improve their output and save time and money in the process.

If you are using Word to write your novels, then the Kindle Create Add-in for newer Office PC versions of Word is an excellent way to quickly create a Kindle eBook and paperback format of your novel and preview the eBook from inside Word.

The best thing to do is experiment and have fun!

Create a new copy of your novel and take an hour to play with the system and find out if Kindle Create works for you and your specific novel.

Any questions? The Kindle Create support team respond very quickly to any questions you may have, no matter how simple. It is their business to support indie authors and get them into print and online as quickly as possible.

Happy publishing!

Kindle Create Publishing: Summary Checklist

Manuscript Preparation

√	Remove all formatting from your text document.
√	Re-Introduce a Simple Normal Text style.
√	Re-Introduce a Simple Chapter Heading 1 style.

Getting Started with Kindle Create

√	Download the Kindle Create Tool.
√	Create a New Project and upload your text document as a .doc(x) file
√	Edit the Automatic Table of Contents list the system generates for your eBook.
√	Select a Theme for your Kindle eBook.

Build a Kindle eBook using Kindle Create

√	**Format the Front Matter/Book Start Elements using the templates.** Start with the Title Page and then work through each of the front matter pages.
√	**Format and Customise the Chapter Title Style.**
√	**Font and Font Size.** Use a Kindle Create theme then edit with formatting.
√	**Spacing after the Chapter Title.**
√	**Create a New Style for the Body Text based on the theme.**
√	**Alignment of the Text.** Should be fully justified (right and left).
√	**Font and Font Size.** At least 11 point to make it easy to read.
√	**First Line of Every Paragraph Indent.** Usually 0.3 to 0.5cm.
√	**Line Spacing in the Text.** Usually 1.2 or 1.3.
√	**Line Spacing between Paragraphs.** Usually 3 to 6 pt.
√	**Format and Customise Scene Separator Symbols - based on the theme.**
√	**Create a New Style for the First Paragraph of Each New Chapter.**
√	**No Indent for the First Paragraph.** Otherwise the same as body text.
√	**Set a Dropped Cap for the First Letter, or Uppercase First Few Words.**
√	**Format the Back Matter/Book End Elements using the templates.**

The Kindle Previewer and Export Tools

√	**Use the Kindle Create Preview tool to check the appearance of your eBook.** Edit your Kindle Create document until you are delighted with the results.
√	**Export your Kindle eBook as a .kpf file which is ready to be uploaded into KDP.**

PART FOUR. YOUR AMAZON AUTHOR PAGE

37

YOUR AMAZON AUTHOR PAGE

The next step is to create your author profile page on the Amazon Author Central platform. You will have to create a separate Amazon Author Central account for each of the Amazon stores where your books are sold. Unfortunately, the information is not shared centrally

For example, go to https://authorcentral.amazon.co.uk/ or https://authorcentral.amazon.com and click '**Join Author Central**' to get started.

Building your Amazon Author Brand
The first thing to do is to create your author biography, including:

• your professional author photo linked to your author brand, together with an author video if you prefer to speak directly to your readers

• your interesting biography and achievements and credentials

• links to your website, blog and social media pages.

This free author page is a powerful way to convey your author brand to any prospective buyer of your book. You can control precisely what your readers will see when they click on your author name on the books you publish.

Add Editorial Advance Reviews of your work
You can **add exclusive 'Editorial' Review content** which Amazon will publish on the Kindle Store page for that book. You can ask for advance readers to provide you with brief testimonials about your book. These reviews help to validate the content and provides social proof that your book is worth a reader's time and money.

Tracking Customer Reviews
You can read all your book reviews from inside your Author Central account.

Tracking your Sales Data

Claim all the books that you have published which are available on the Amazon store for each pen name that you use. When your eBook goes live on Amazon you can **add that eBook to your author profile.**

I usually search for my author pen name. Simply click on the **This is my book** button to add this book to your profile bibliography. If you are published in translation, then it is always a good idea to click on the book link and check that you are the author.

When your books are loaded you can then track the sales data.

For example. For authorcentral.amazon.com you can track the sales data for every eBook and paperback that you have claimed in the system. BookScan data tracks weekly sales and sales by geography, while your sales rank charts out the entire sales history of each book in graphical form.

amazon Author Central   Author Page   Books   Sales Info ~   Customer Reviews

NPD BookScan
Sales Rank

Welcome to Author Central

We encourage you to add or update information about yourself for your Amazon Author Page. Here's some quick links to important places:

- **Update your Author Page**
  - Add multimedia, blog feeds, or events to an Amazon Author Page
  - View and edit our list of your books
  - Add a book to your bibliography

In contrast, authorcentral.amazon.co.uk only provides the Amazon sales rank graphs for your books so there are geographical differences between the author profile accounts.

amazon Author Central   Author Page   Books   **Sales Rank**   Customer Reviews

Using Author Central to Market your books

• Amazon provides an author page URL website address that you can use to take readers straight to your Amazon author page from your email signature or other promotion.

• You can also ask readers to click on the "Follow" button on your profile and they will be alerted by email when you have a new release. Amazon does your marketing for you!

• If you have the book on pre-order, you can still claim your book inside your author central account, add advance review comments and link to the book description page in your book launch promotional materials.

I would recommend taking the time to learn how to maximise your use of author central and treat it as a free author website on the biggest online bookstore in the world.

PART FIVE. BOX SETS

38

CREATING A BOX SET OF BOOKS

If you have a backlist of eBooks or print books, a box set is an excellent way of creating an additional income stream and provide great value to the reader compared to the price of the individual titles.

The idea is simple. You combine the manuscripts of three or more books which are linked in some way into collections and publish them as one single book.

This can apply to both eBooks and print on demand paperback print books, although with print books you should make it clear to readers that they are going to receive the box set compilation as one printed book, not a collection of separate printed books.

For example. Many genre fiction writers prefer to write series of books set in the same story world or location, then offer box sets of earlier books in the series at a lower price.

Non-fiction authors may create a series of books covering specific aspects of one topic, which could also be of interest to readers as a box set compilation.

The Box Set Table of Contents

Ideally you should create a new Table of Contents for the box set so that you can separate out the books, and not repeat end matter such as the author section in every book.

The Box Set Book Cover

Some box set publishers ask their cover designer to create a 3-D cover for the Amazon book page for the box set. This can be successful for eBooks, but not for print.

In all cases, you should format and upload the box set as a new book, with a new title, into KDP following the standard instructions we have already covered in earlier chapters.

THANK YOU!

Thank you for reading **HOW TO PUBLISH A BOOK ON AMAZON.**

I hope that you enjoyed this book in a new series supporting indie authors.

I love sharing my experience and information with other independent publishers like myself who are looking for the best way to share their work online, but struggle with the overwhelming amount of information out there right now.

If you enjoyed this book and found it useful, I would really appreciate it if you would consider leaving a review of this book, no matter how short, at the retailer site where you bought your copy or on sites like Goodreads.

YOU are the key to this book's success.

I read every review and they really do make a huge difference.

Reviews help other readers to discover the kind of books and guides they want to read and is a great way to support authors. Thank You!

More Guides BY NINA HARRINGTON

You can discover more at NinaHarrington.com.

KINDLE CREATE FOR FICTION AUTHORS

<u>A NEW ONLINE COURSE</u>

I know that many authors prefer to see the training material live on screen, so I have recorded an online course with live video demonstrations on how to use Kindle Create.

Most of the course material is based on the content of this book with added screen capture videos.

FIND OUT MORE HERE :>>>

https://www.udemy.com/kindle-create-for-fiction-authors

ABOUT THE AUTHOR

Nina Harrington grew up in rural Northumberland, England and decided aged eleven that her dream job was to be a librarian because then she could read all the books in the public library whenever she wanted!

Many years later she took the bold decision to take a career break from working in the pharmaceutical industry to realise her dream of being a fiction writer. No contract, no cash, but a compelling passion for the written word.

Nina writes fun, award-winning contemporary romance for HarperCollins, including the Mills and Boon Modern Tempted and Harlequin KISS lines plus single title romantic mysteries. She also self-publishes guides and training courses for authors.

Over 1.6 million of her books have been sold in 28 countries and translated into 23 languages.

Nina is the founder of TheProlificAuthor.com and Fast-Track Guides.

When she is not creating stories which make her readers smile, or researching best practices for authorpreneurs, her hobbies are cooking, eating, enjoying good wine, and talking, for which she has had specialist training.

Find out more about Nina at: https://ninaharrington.com/